George Washington, Worthington Chauncey Ford

Wills of George Washington and His Immediate Ancestors

George Washington, Worthington Chauncey Ford

Wills of George Washington and His Immediate Ancestors

ISBN/EAN: 9783744661713

Printed in Europe, USA, Canada, Australia, Japan

Cover: Foto ©ninafisch / pixelio.de

More available books at **www.hansebooks.com**

WILLS

OF

GEORGE WASHINGTON

AND HIS

IMMEDIATE ANCESTORS.

EDITED BY

WORTHINGTON CHAUNCEY FORD.

BROOKLYN, N. Y.:
HISTORICAL PRINTING CLUB.
1891.

250 Copies Printed.
No. 196

CONTENTS.

	PAGE
WILL OF JOHN WASHINGTON, 1675	7
POWER OF ATTORNEY, BY ANN WASHINGTON, 1698	19
WILL OF LAWRENCE WASHINGTON, 1675	21
WILL OF LAWRENCE WASHINGTON, 1698	31
WILL OF AUGUSTINE WASHINGTON, 1743	39
EDMUND PENDLETON TO GEORGE WASHINGTON, 3 JULY, 1769	53
WILL OF MARY BALL, 1788	59
GEORGE WASHINGTON TO BETTY LEWIS, 13 SEPTEMBER, 1789	63
GEORGE WASHINGTON TO BETTY LEWIS, 12 OCTOBER, 1789	68
GEORGE WASHINGTON TO BURGES BALL AND CHARLES CARTER, 18 OCTOBER, 1789	69
WILL OF LAWRENCE WASHINGTON, 1752	71
WILL OF GEORGE WASHINGTON, 1799	81
GEORGE WASHINGTON TO DAVID STUART, 15 JANUARY, 1788	141
WILL OF BUSHROD WASHINGTON, 1826	149
WILL OF JOHN AUGUSTINE WASHINGTON, 1822	173
WILL OF JOHN CUSTIS, 1708	183
INDEX	199

NOTE.

I HAVE obtained copies of the wills of the immediate ancestors of George Washington, and print them with certain others, as matters of personal as well as historical interest. The wills of John, the immigrant, and of George Washington, are taken from the originals; the others are from certified copies, made by the custodians of the originals. I have followed the MSS. closely, adding a few notes, in which I have received great assistance from Rev. Horace Edwin Hayden, of Wilkesbarre, Pa.

WORTHINGTON CHAUNCEY FORD.

Brooklyn, May, 1891.

THE

WILL

OF

JOHN WASHINGTON,

GREAT-GRANDFATHER OF

GEORGE WASHINGTON.

IN the name [of] god amen. I John washington of washington parish* in y͠e Countie of westmerland† in Virginie gent, being of good & perfect

---

* In the session of March 1655–6 the Assembly directed that all counties not already divided into parishes should be so divided by the next county court, as the "improvident saveing" of those who had neglected to do this, made the inhabitants "loose the greatest benefitt and comfort a Christian can have, by hearing the word and vse of the blessed sacraments." *Hening*, I., 400. The act was repeated in March 1657–8, and it must have been under one of these that Washington parish was laid off. In 1724 the parish was about thirty miles in length, five in breadth, and contained about 200 hundred families. There were two churches in it, one called the Round Hill church, and the annual salary of the minister 16,000 pounds of tobacco. "The gentleman who bequeathed my Glebe to the parish [William Horton, his will bore date 10 January, 1700], left the whole tract (containing 440 acres), to be disposed of by the vestry for the better maintenance of a minister and schoolmaster, the Vestry made no division of the land, but gave it to me as a glebe, with this proviso, that I provide a sufficient person to instruct the youth in reading, writing and arithmetic under my inspection, which condition I have complied with." *Lawrence De Butts, minister of Washington Parish in* 1724. Printed in Perry, *Church in Virginia*, 292. The glebe was directed to be sold in 1778.

† The first mention of Westmoreland county is found in the Randolph *MS.*, where in 1653, in the fourth year of the commonwealth, its bounds were laid off "ffrom Machoactoke river where Mr. Cole lives: And so vpwards to the ffalls of the great river of Pawtomake above the Necostins towne." *Hening*, memory,

memory, thankes be unto Almighty god (for it) & Calling to remembrance the uncertaine estate of this trans[itory] life, & that all flesh must yield unto death, when it shall plea[se] god for to Call, doe make Constitute ordaine & declare this my last will & testament in maner & forme following, reuoaking & anulling by thes presents all & euery testament & testa[ments], will & wills heirtofore by me made & Declared [either by word] or by writeing & [these?] be taken only for my last will & testament & noe other, & first being hartily sorry from the bottome of my hart for my sins past, most humbly desireing forgiueness of the same from the Almighty god (my sauiour) & redeimer, in whome & by the meritts of Jesus Christ, I trust & belieue assuredly to be saued, & to haue full remission & forgiueness of all my sins & y^t my soule wth my body at the generall day of ressurrection shall arise againe wth joy & through the merrits of Christ death & passion posses & inherit the Kingdom of heauen, prepared for his ellect & Chossen & my body to be buried in ye plantation wheire I now

---

I., 381. The first session in which Burgesses sat for Westmoreland was that of November, 1654, when John Holland and Alexander Baynham were the representatives. In the session of October, 1666, Col. Nicholas Spencer and Col. John Washington appeared as the representatives. In 1675 the two men were associated again, with others, to deal with the Indians. *Hening*, II., 331.

liue,

liue, by the side of my wife* y̩t is already buried & two Children of mine & now for the setling of my temporall estate & such goods Chatles & debts as it hath pleased god far aboue my Deserts, to bestow uppon me I doe giue & dispose the same in maner & forme following—

first I will y̩t all those debts & duties y̩t I owe in right or Conscience to any maner of person or persons w̩t soever shall be well & truly Contented & payd or ordained to be payd by my executors— †
* * *

Inprimis I giue & bequeath unto my eldest sonne [   ] ington y̩t seat of land wheiron Henery flagg   ] watts & Robert Hedges, being by patten &   being by my father pope made ouer to me & my heirs lawfully begotten of my body—

Item I give unto my soñ Lawrence washington my watter Mill w̩th all appertinances & Land belonging to it a[t] the head of Rosiers Creik to him & his heirs foreuer, reseruing to my wife her thirds durring her Life.

Item I giue unto my soñ Lawrence washington y̩t seate of Land w̩ch I bought of M̩r Lewis Maruim, being about two hundred & fifty acres, at the mouth of rosiers Crieck on y̩e north west side, w̩th all the

---
* Anne Pope.
† Three or four words illegible.

houseing

houseing theirunto belonging to him & his heirs for euer reserueing to my wife her thirds durring her Life—

Item I giue unto my soñ Lawrence washington y^t seat of Land at upper Machotock wch I bought of Mr Anthony Bridge & Mr John Rosier being about nine hundred acres to him & his heirs foreuer, reserueing to my wife her thirds durring her life.

Item I giue unto my soñ Lawrence washington my halfe & share of fiue thousand acres of land in Stafford * County wch is betwixt Coll Nicolas spencer & myselfe wch we are engaged y^t there shall be no benifit taken by suruiuour ship, to him & his heirs foreuer. †

---

* Stafford County is first mentioned in a law of 1666, providing that each county provide a weaver and loom at its own expense. In 1730 a part was taken from Stafford and King George Counties to form Prince William County. Twelve years later Prince William was divided; the western part retained the name of Prince William, and the eastern became Fairfax County, the parish of Truro.

† The patent was issued by Thos. Culpepper, 1 March, 1674, and conveyed to Col. Nicholas Spencer and Lieut. Col. John Washington, "five thousand acres of land scituate Lying and being within the said terrytory in-the County of Stafford in the ffreshes of Pottomooke River and neere oppositt to Piscatoway Indian Towne in Mariland and neere the Land of Capt. Giles on the North side, and neere the Land surveyed for Mr. Wm. Grein Mr. Wm. Dudley and others on the south side; being a necke of Land bounded betwixt two Creeks and the

Item

Item I doe giue unto my son Johne washington y.^t plantation whereon I now liue wch I bought of Dauid Anderson y.^t plantation next to Mr John [Foxall?] y.^t I bought (wch was Ric. Hills) to him & his heirs for euer & y.^t seate of Land of about four hundred acres wch Lyeth uppon ye Head of Rappahanecke Creike & adjoyning uppon David norways orphants Land the Land being formerly John Whittsons &   to me, to him & his heirs for euer, reserueing to my wife her thirds of the afoure sayd Land during her Life.

Maine River, on the East p'te   by the said Main River of Pottomooke, on the North p'te by a Creeke Called by the English Little Hunting Creeke and the maine Branch thereof on the south p'te by a Creeke named and Called by the Indians Epsewasson Creeke and the maine Branch thereof which Creeke devides this Land of Gren and Dudley and others on the west p'te by a right Lyne drawn from the Branches of the aforesaid Epsewasson and Little Hunting Creeke."

In the Virginia State Land Registry, No. 6, p. 615, is recorded a grant to Lt. Col. John Washington, of 5,000 acres in Stafford County, 1677.

Nicholas Spencer survived Washington, and served in the Governor's Council after 1680, as President, and also as Secretary of the Colony in 1683. Mr. Hayden tells me he was a justice in Westmoreland County in 1699, and married Miss Mottrom, daughter of John Mottrom.

Nicholas Spencer devised his moiety of this tract to his son Francis Spencer and his heirs forever. Capt. Lawrence Washington was one of the feoffees in trust under Spencer's will, dated 25 April, 1688, and received forty shillings for a mourning ring. *Henry F. Waters' Gleanings.*

Item

Item I giue unto my soñ John washington yt seate of Land wch Robert foster now liueth on being about three hundred acres* to him & his heirs foreuer, Likewise I give unto my sayd son John washington yt seat of Land wch Robert Richards liueth on wch I had of my bro: Lawrence washington being about three hundred & fifty acres to him & his heirs for euer reserueing to my wife her thirds of the two sayd tracts of Land during her Life—†

Item I giue & bequeath unto my daughter Añ washington yt seate of Land yt tract of Land yt Tho: Jordan now liueth on being about twelve hundred acres‡ to her & her heirs for euer, likewise I giue & bequeath unto my sayd Daughter that tract of Land whereon John fries‖ now liueth being about fourteen hundred acres after Mr fr ke hath his quantitie out of it to her & her

---

* Perhaps the 300 acres in Northumberland County, granted to Major John Washington, 1 June, 1664. Virginia State Land Registry, No. 5, p. 49.

† In the Virginia State Land Registry, No. 6, p. 60, is recorded a grant of 700 acres in Stafford County, to Lawrence Washington and Robert Richards, 27 September, 1667.

‡ A tract of this size was granted, 4 September, 1661, to Major John Washington and Thomas Pope. It lay in Westmoreland County. Virginia State Land Registry, No. 5, p. 54.

Ann married Major Francis Wright. He was justice in Westmoreland, 1699.

‖ Or *Frier*.

heirs

heirs for euer reserueing to my wife her thirds of the two above seates durring her Life.

Item I giue unto my sayd Daughter, wch was her mother's desire & my promise ye Cash in ye new parlour & the Diamond ring & her mother's rings & the white quilt & the white Curtains & vallians—

And as for the rest of my personall estate after my debts & dues are sattisfied justly wh^{ch} I desire should be sattisfied out of my [ ] Cropps, which I doe not question but will be far more than I doe owe (thankes be unto god for it) theirfore it is my desire y^t my estate should not Come to any appraisement, but I order & bequeath a[s] followeth y^t is to say that their shall be a just Inuentory & List taken of my personall estate y^t I am possessed of & for to be deuided in quantitie & quallitie, by three men of Judgement wch I request the Court to nominate, into foure [parts] to be equall & proportionable deuided in quantitie & qualitie the [one] fourth part I giue to my Loueing wife in kind in lew of her dower or [claime], & one fourth part to my soñ Lawrence washington in kind, and one fourth part to my soñ John washington in kind, & one fourth part to my daughter Añ washington in kind to them & either of them seuerally and their heirs for euer & it is my will y^t if either my aboue sayd children should happen to dy, before they obtaine the age of one & twenty yeares or day of mariadge, then the Land of y^t child y^t Dieth
to be

to be the eldest soñ then Liueing, & if both my soñs should dy then the Land to be my daughter Añ, & as for the personall estate if any of my three Children should happen to dy, before they Come of age or day of mariadge, then it is my will that the two suruiueing children should equally deuide the personall estate of ye child y^t is dead betwixt them and theirs for euer.

Item I giue and bequeath after all my legacies payd out w^t mony I shall haue in England to my soñ Lawrence washington.

Item my desire is y^t their may be a funerall sermon preached at ye church & that their be no other funerall kept y^t will exceed four thousand pounds of tobacco.

Item I giue unto the Lower Church of washington parish [ ] ten Comandments and the Kings armes wch is my desire should be sent for out of w^t mony I haue in England.

Item it is my desire y^t w^t estate I shall dy possessed should be kept intire wthout deuideing untill all debts & dues be payd & sattisfied.

Item I giue unto my bro: Lawrence washington four thousand pounds of tobb^{co} & Caske.

Item I giue unto my nephew John washington my godson eldest soñ to my bro: Lawrence washington one young mare of two years old.

Item it is my desire y^t when my estate is deuided in quantitie & qualitie into foure equall parts & y^t

& y:t my wife hath taken her fourth part, y:t then euery Childs part should be put put* uppon their towne † plant [ ] or plantations theire for to be managed to the best aduantage for the bringing up & [educating each child] according to the proffit of each Children's share.

Item it is my desire y:t my wife should haue the bringing up of my daughter Añ washington untill my soñ Lawrence comes to age or her day of mariadge & my wife for to haue the manadgement of her part to my daughter's best aduantadge.

Item I doe giue to my bro: Thomas Pope teñ pounds out of y:e mony I haue in England.

Item I doe giue unto my sister Marthaw Washington teñ pounds out of y:e mony I haue in England & w:t soeuer else she shall be oweing to me for transporteing herselfe into this Country—& a year's accomodation after her Comeing in & four thousand pounds of tobb:co & Caske.

Item it is my desire y:t my bro: M:r Thomas Pope haue the bringing up of my soñ John Washington & for to haue the manadgement of his estate to my soñs best aduantadge untill [he] be of age of one & twenty yeares or day of mariadge—

finally I doe ordaine & appoint my bro: M:r Lawrence washington & my soñ Lawrence washington & my Loueing wife M:rs Añ washington my

---

* Or *out*. † Or *owne*.
whole

whole & soale executors of this my Last will & testament as witness my hand & seale this 21ˢᵗ of 7ber 1675.

JOHN WASHINGTON.

Signed & sealed in yᵉ
   presence of us
     JOHN LORD.*
     JOHN APPLETON.

Yé 10th Jana: 1677

Then this will was proved by yᵉ oath of Capᵃ Jnº Lord, Capᵃ Jnº Appleton being decsᵈ † recorded in yᵉ County Court records of WestmorLd.

---

* John Lord was appointed a Commissioner for Westmoreland, 1660. He was [1661-2] ordered with others to pay for injuries done to Wahanganoche, king of the Potowmack Indians; refusing to do this, he was fined and suspended from office. This made the commission for Westmoreland so small, that Westmoreland and Northumberland were joined under one commission.

† Died in 1676.

POWER OF ATTORNEY BY THE WIDOW OF JOHN WASHINGTON.

Know all men by these presents that I Mrs. Ann Washington Widow & Relict of Capt John Washington of Westmoreland County decd, do hereby constitute, appoint and ordain my trusty and well beloved friend Mr. Caleb Butler* of the said County my true and Lawfull Attorney for me and in my name, and to my use, to ask, sue, receive and recover of all person or Persons whatsoever living, residing & abiding within this Colony of Virginia or province of Maryland, all such sum or sums of money, or Tobacco which shall be made appear to be due to me whether by bill, bond or Book account or otherways & upon non-payment of any part of the above Tobacco or money by any person or persons whatsoever I do impower him the said Caleb Butler to arrest & implead and into prison cast all such person or persons as he sees fitt, and out of Prison to release & sett free at his pleasure and acquittance or other discharges to give for me & in my name and for my use, and likewise I give my said attorney full power to employ any one attorney or more if he sees fit, and to discharge them at his

---

* A justice in Westmoreland, 1699. *Hayden.*

pleasure

pleasure & to act and do in all my affairs belonging to me in Virginia or Maryland as if I myself were personally present, ratifying and allowing & confirming all and whatsoever my said attorney shall act and do in the premises. As Witness my hand and seale this 28th day of March 1698.

ANN WASHINGTON. [SEAL.]

Sealed Signed & Delivered in presence of,
THOMAS HOWES,
HENRY WICKEFF.

WESTMORELAND Sct:

At a Court held for the Said County the 30th day of March 1698.

The above Letter of attorney was proved by the oaths of the Witnesses thereto subscribed and ordered to be recorded.- Teste

JAMES WESTCOMB C. W. C.*

---

*From *The Nation*, 18 December, 1890.

THE WILL

OF

LAWRENCE WASHINGTON

(EMIGRANT.)

In the name of God, Amen.

I, Lawrence Washington, of the county of Rappac.,* being sick and weak in body, but of sound and perfect memory, do make and ordain this, my last will and testament, hereby *revoking*, *annulling*, and making void all former wills and *Codicells*, heretofore by me made, either by word or writing, and this only to be taken for my last will and testament.

Imprs. I give and bequeath my *Soule* into the hands of Almighty God, hoping and trusting through the mercy of Jesus Christ, my one *Savior* and redeemer, to receive full pardon and forgiveness of all my *sinns*, and my body to the earth, to be buried in comely and decent manner, by my Executrix hereafter named, and for my worldly goods, I thus *dispose* them. Item, I give and bequeath unto my loving daughter, Mary Washington,† my whole estate in England, both *reall* and *personall*, to her and the heirs of her body, law-

---

* Rappahannock county was laid off from the upper part of Lancaster in 1656. In 1692 the county was divided into Richmond and Essex.

† Mary Washington was a daughter of the first wife, Mary Jones,—the only issue of the marriage.

fully

fully begotten, forever, to be delivered into her possession *immediately* after my decease, by my Executrix hereafter named. I give and bequeath unto my aforesaid daughter, Mary Washington, my smallest stone ring and one silver cup, now in my possession, to her and her heirs, forever, to be delivered to her *immediately* after my decease. I give and bequeath unto my loving son, John Washington,* all my bookes, to him and his heirs, forever, to be delivered to him when he shall come to the age of Twenty-one *yeares*. I give and bequeath unto my son, John, and daughter, Ann Washington, all the rest of my plate, but what is before *exprest* to be equally divided between them, and delivered into their possession when they come of age. Item, my will is, that all my debts which of right and justice I owe to any man be justly and truly paid, as *allso* my funerall expenses, after which my will is, that all my whole estate, both *reall* and *personall*, be equally divided between my loving wife, Jane Washington,† and the two chil-

---

* Married Mary Townshend. "She was daughter of Col. Robert and Mary (Langhorne) Townshend. Her sister Frances, married Francis Dade. In 1727 Mary (Townshend) Washington conveyed part of the Townshend patent of 1850 to her son John." *Hayden.*

† Jane Fleming. "I have long thought that Lawrence Washington married a *widow* Joyce Fleming. 'Aug. 19, 1660, Alex. Fleming and wife Ursula made deed in Rapp^k Co.' 'Feb. 6,

dren God

dren God hath given me by her Vizt. John and Ann Washington. I give and bequeath it all to them, and the *heires* of their bodies, lawfully begotten, forever, my *sonn's* part to be delivered to him when

---

167½, Lawrence Washington and wife *Joyce* conveyed 200 acres formerly Capt. Alex. Fleming's, by him assigned to Jno. Thomazine, and by T. assigned to Lawrence Washington.'
'In 1692, Thomas Pace and wife Jane, Rowland Thornton and wife Elizabeth, one of the daughters of Alex. Fleming, *deceased*, deeded 320 acres, part of 960, given by Fleming to his wife and two daughters, which 320 came to Pace with Alexia his former wife.' It seems as if Alex. Fleming married (1) Ursula; (2) Joyce, who married (2) Lawrence Washington, and (3) ——." *Hayden.*

Among the *Washington Papers* I found a copy of a letter written by the son of Lawrence Washington, to his half sister Mary, then residing in England. I give it in full:

VIRGINIA, JUNE Y^E 22^D, 1699.

Dear & Loving Sister,

I had the happiness to see a Letter which you sent to my Aunt Howard, who died about a year and a half ago; I had heard of you by her before, but could not tell whether you were alive or not. It was truly great joy to hear that I had such a relation alive as yourself; not having any such a one by my Father's side as yourself. My Father had one Daughter by my Mother, who died when she was very young, before my remembrance. My Mother had three Daughters when my Father married her, one died last winter, and left four or five children, the other two are alive & married and have had several children. My Mother married another man after my Father, who spent all, so that I had not the value of twenty shillings of my Father's Estate, I being the youngest & there-
he come

he come of age, and my daughter's part when she comes of age or day of marriage, which shall first happen. Item, my will is, that that land which became due to me in right of my wife, lying on the South Side of the river, formerly belonging to Capt. Alexander Fleming,* and commonly known by the name of West Falco, be sold by my Executrix hereafter named, for the payment of my debts, immediately after my decease. Item, my will is, that the land I have formerly *entred* with Capt. Wm. Mosely,† be forthwith after my decease, sur-

---

fore the weakest, which generally comes off short. But I thank God my Fortune has been pretty good since, as I have got a kind and loving wife, by whom I have had three sons and a daughter, of which I have buried my daughter and one son. I am afraid I shall never have the happiness of seeing you, since it has pleased God to set us at such a distance, but hoping to hear from you by all opportunities, which you shall assuredly do from him that is,

Your ever loving Brother
till death

Jno. WASHINGTON.

If you write to me direct yours to me in Stafford county, on Potomack River in Virginia. Vale.

To Mrs. Mary Gibson, living at Hawnes in Bedf's. These sent with care.

* A vestryman and justice in 1675. *Hayden.*

† William Mosely was associated with Col. John Washington and others in 1673, in settling the bounds between the Counties of Northumberland and Lancaster. *Hening*, II., 309. The

veyed

veyed and *pattented* by my Execx. hereafter named, and if it shall amount to the quantity of one thousand acres, then I give and bequeath unto Alexander Barrow, two hundred acres of the sd. land, to him and his heires, forever, the remainder I give and bequeath unto my loving wife afores'd and two children, to them and their heires, forever, to be equally *divided* between them. Item, my will is, that if it shall please God to take my daughter Mary out of the world before she comes of age, or have heirs lawfully begotten of her body, then I give and bequeath my land in England, which by my will I have given to her, unto my son, John Washington and his heirs, and the personall estate which I have given to her, I give and bequeath the same unto my daughter, Ann Washington and her heires, forever. Item, I do hereby make and ordain my loving wife, Jane Washington, Executrix of this my last will and testament, to see it performed, and I do hereby make and appoint my dear and *loveing* Brother Coll John Washington, and my *loveing* friend Thomas Hawkins (in case of the death or neglect of my executrix), to be the overseers and guardians of my Children *untill* they come of age to the truth whereof I have hereunto

---

house of William Mosely, Senr., is mentioned in the act for dividing Lower Norfolk county. *Hening*, III., 95. He was a justice in Essex, 1699. *Hayden.*

Sett

Sett my hand and *Seale*, this 27th of September, 1675.

LAWRENCE WASHINGTON. [SEAL.]

Signed Sealed and declared to be
his last will and testament,
in the presence of us.

CORNELIUS WOOD.
JOHN B. BARROW,
HENRY SANDY, Junr.

A codicil of the last will and testament of Lawrence Washington, annexed to his will, and made September 27th, 1675.

Item, my will is, that my part of the land I now live upon, which became due to me by marriage of my wife, I leave it wholy and solely to her disposable after my decease, as witness my hand, the day and year above written.

LAWRENCE WASHINGTON. [SEAL.]

Signed Sealed and declared to be
a Codicil of my last will and testament, in the *presence* of us.

CORNELIUS WOOD,
HENRY SANDY, Junr.

The above named Henry Sandy, Junr. aged 70 *veares*, or thereab'ts, sworn and examined, saith, that he did see the above named Lawrence Washington, Sign, Seale and publish the above mentioned, to be his last will and testament, and that he
was in

was in perfect sence and memory at the Signing, Sealing and publishing thereof, to the best of your deponent's Judgment. HENRY SANDY.

Juratus est Henricus Sandy, in Cur. Com. Rappkac. Sexto die, Jany, Año 1677. Jr Saca end pr and probat.
Sc st

EDMD CRASK, Cl Cy.

A Copy, Teste
  James Roy Micou, Clerk,
    Essex County Court,
      State of Virginia.*

---

* I have taken this from that inexpressibly silly book, Welles' *Pedigree and History of the Washington Family*. The will agrees with the summary printed by Bishop Meade, and is accepted by Mr. William H. Whitmore.

THE WILL

OF

LAWRENCE WASHINGTON,

GRANDFATHER OF

GEORGE WASHINGTON.

IN the Name of God amen I Lawrence Washington of Washington Parish in the County of Westmoreland in Virginia, Gentleman, being of Good and perfect memory, thanks be unto Almighty God for it & calling to mind the uncertain Estate of this Transitory life & that all Flesh must yield unto death when it shall please God to call me doe make constitute, ordain & Declare this my last will, and Testament in manner and form following, revoking and annulling by these presents all and every Testament and Testaments, will or wills heretofore by me made and declared either by word or writing & this to be taken only for my last will and Testament and none other, and first being heartily sorry from the bottom of my heart for my sins, most humbly desireing forgiveness of the same from the Almighty God my saviour & Redeemer, in whome by the merits of Jesus Christ, I Trust and believe assuredly to be saved and to have full remission & forgiveness of all my sins and that my soal with my body at the General day of Resurrection shall rise again with Joy, and through the Merits of Christs Death and passion, possess & Inherit the Kingdom of Heaven prepared for his Elect & chosen and my body to be buried if please God I depart in this County of Westmoreland, by the side the side of my Father and Mother & neare my Brothers & Sisters & my children, and now for the setling of my Temporal Estate and such goods, Chattles and debts as it hath pleased God far above my desarts to bestow upon me I doe ordain give and bequeath the same in manner and form following: Imprimis I [will] that all those Debts and dues that I owe in right or Conscience to any manner of Person or Persons whatsoever shall be well contented & paid or ordained or demanded to be paid by my Executors or Extx: hereafter named. Item I give and bequeath to my well beloved friends Mr. William Thompson clk & Mr. Samuel Thompson each of them a mourning Ring of Thirty shillings value each ring: Item I give and bequeath to my Godson Lawrence Butler one young mare & two cows: Item I give and bequeath to my sister Anne Writts* children one man servant a piece of four or five years to serve or Three Thousand pounds of Tobacco to purchase the same, to be delivered or paid to them when they arrive to the age of Twenty years old: Item I give and bequeath to my sister Lewis† a morning Wring of forty shillings price: Item I give to my Cuz: John Washington Sen: of Stafford County all my wearing apparel:

---

* See note on page 14.

† John Lewis married a sister of Mrs. Washington—Elizabeth Warner.

Item

Item I give unto my Cozen John Washington's Eldest son Lawrence Washington my Godson one man servant of four or five years to serve or Three Thousand pounds of Tobacco to purchase the same: to be paid him when he comes to the age of Twenty one yeare old: Item I give to my godsons Lawrence Butler & Lewis Nicholas that Tract of Land joining upon Meridah Edwards and Daniel White, being Two hundred and seventy five acres of Land to be equally divided between them and their heirs forever: Item I give to the upper and Lower Churches of Washington parish each of them a Pulpett cloth & cushion: Item it is my will to have a Funeral sermon at the church, and to have none other Funeral to exceed Three Thousand pounds of Tobacco. Item it is my will after my Debts & Legacies are paid, that my personal Estate be equally divided into four parts: my loving Wife Mildred Washington* to have one part, my son John Washington to have another part, my son Augustin Washington to have another Part, and my Daughter Mildred Washington† to have the other part: to be delivered to them in specie when they shall come to the age of Twenty one years old. Item I give to my son [John] Washington this seat

---

* Mildred, Daughter of Col. Augustine Warner.

† Mildred was twice married: 1. Roger Gregory; 2. Col. Henry Willis.

of Land

of Land where I now live, and that whole tract of Land Lying from the mouth of Machodack extending to a place called the round hills, with the addition I have thereunto made of William Webb and William Rush to him and heirs forever. Item I give and bequeath unto my Son Augustine Washington all the dividend of Land that I bought of Mr. Robert Liston's Children in England Lying in Mattox, between my Brother & Mr. Balridges Land, where Mr. Daniel Liston formerly lived, by Estimation 400 acres to him and his heirs forever,* as Likewise that Land that was Richard Hills: Item I give and bequeath unto my said Son Augustine Washington, all that Tract of Land where Mr. Lewis Markham now lives after the said Markhams & his now wife's decease, by estimation 700 acres more or less to him and his heirs forever: Item I give and bequeath my daughter Mildred Washington all my Land in Stafford County, Lying upon hunting Creek where Mrs. Elizabeth Minton & Mrs. Williams now lives by Estimation 2500 acres to her and her heirs forever.† Item I

---

*This Liston tract was Wakefield, the birthplace of George Washington. *George Washington and Mount Vernon*, xxv. A very careful survey of this place was issued by the United States Coast and Geodetic Survey in 1879.

†The Mount Vernon tract. Roger and Mildred Gregory gave a release, 17 May, 1726, to Augustine Washington, for 2500 acres of the Mount Vernon tract, and 18 October, 1726, a lease and release for the land was executed.

give

give my water mill to my son John Washington to him and his heirs forever: Item it is my will and desire if either of my children should die before they come to age or day of marriage, his or her personal estate be equally divided between the two survivors and their Mother: Item it is my will and desire if all my Children should die before they come of age or day of Marriage, that my Brother's children shall enjoy all their Estate real, Except that Land that I bought of Mr. Robert Liston's children, which I give to my loving wife and her heirs forever, and the rest as aforesaid to them and their heirs forever: Item I give my personall Estate in case of all my childrens death as abovesaid, to be equally divided between my Wife and Brother's children, my wife to have the one-half: Item I give that Land which I bought of my Brother Francis Wright, being 200 acres lying near Storkes Quarter, to my son John Washington and his heirs for ever: Item It is my desire that my [estate] should not be appraised but kept intire and delivered them as above given according to time & my Children to continue under the care & Tuition of their Mother, till they come of age or day of marriage, and she to have the profits of their Estates towards the bringing of them up and Keeping them at School: Item I doe ordain and appoint my Cozen John Washington of Stafford and my friend Mr. Samuel Thompson my Executors, and my my loving wife Mildred Washington my Executrix of this my last Will & Testament. In Witness whereof I have hereunto set my hand and seale this 11th day of March Anno Dom 1697/8.

LAWRENCE WASHINGTON. [Seal.]

Signed Seald declared & pronounced in presence of us,

>ROBT REDMAN,
>GEORGE WEEDON,
>THOMAS HOWES,
>JOHN ROSIER.

WESTMORELAND Sct:

At a Court held for the said County the 30th day of March 1698.

The last will and Testament of Lawrence Washington Gent deced within written was proved by the oaths of George Weedon Thomas Howes & John Rosier Three of the witnesses thereof subscribed, and a probate thereof Granted to Samuel Thompson one of the Executors therein named, and the Will ordered to be recorded.

Teste

JAMES WESTCOMB, C. W. C.

THE WILL

OF

AUGUSTINE WASHINGTON,

FATHER OF

GEORGE WASHINGTON.

IN the Name of God Amen. I Augustine Washington of the County of King George Gent, being sick and weak but of perfect and disposing sence and memory do make my last Will and Testament in manner follòwing hereby Revoking all former Will or Wills whatsoever by me heretofore made

IMPRIMIS I give unto my son Lawrence Washington & his heirs forever, all that Plantation and Tract of Land at Hunting Creek in the County of Prince William Containing by Estimation Two Thousand five hundred acres with the water mill adjoyning thereto or lying near the same. And all the slaves, Cattle & Stocke of all kinds whatsoever and all the houshold Furniture whatsoever now in & upon or which have been Commonly possessed by my said son Together with the said Plantation Tract of Land and Mill.

ITEM I Give unto my son Augustine Washington* and his heirs for ever all my Lauds in the County of Westmoreland except such only as are hereinafter otherwise disposed of. Together with Twenty five head of Neat Cattle forty hogs Twenty sheep and a Negro Man named Frank besides those negroes formerly given him by his Mother.

ITEM I Give unto my said son Augustine three

---

* Married Ann Aylett.

young

young working slaves to be purchased for him out of the first profits of the Iron works after my Decease.

ITEM I give unto my son George Washington and his heirs the Land I now Live on which I purchased of the Executrix of Mr. Wm. Strother dec'd.* and one Moiety of my Land lying on Deep Run and Ten Negro Slaves.

ITEM I give unto my son Samuel Washington and his heirs my Land at Chotank in the County of Stafford Containing about six hundred acres †

---

* Two hundred and eighty acres, purchased by Augustine Washington of Margaret Grant, Executrix of William Strother, 3 November, 1738. *Conway.*

† A tract of land, "containing five hundred and thirty-three acres, more or less, called and known by the name of Chotank," was devised by will (1698) of John Withers to his daughter Sarah, during her life, and after her decease, to his cousin William Withers, and the heirs male of his body. In default of such heirs, the land was to go to Thomas Withers, of Lancaster, in Great Britain, and his heir male. William never married, and Thomas, dying in England, the land went to his eldest son Edmund Withers, and at his death passed to his brother William. By his death the title became vested in his son Thomas, who died leaving a son William. In the meantime Sarah had lived upon the place, married Christopher Conoway, and, after his death, conveyed the land to Augustine Washington (12 June, 1727). By his will he left it to his son Samuel, but apparently doubted his complete title, for he provides an equivalent in case the land was not yielded to Samuel. William Withers did dispute the title, and Augustine paid him £600 current money of the colony to quiet Withers' claim, and the Assembly by special act gave a full possession to Samuel and his heirs. *Hening's Statutes,* vi., 513.

and also

and also the other moiety of my Land lying on Deep Run.

ITEM I give unto my son John Washington* and his heirs my Land at the head of Maddox in the County of Westmoreland Containing about seven hundred acres.

ITEM I give unto my son Charles Washington† and his heirs the Land I purchased of my son Lawrence Washington (whereon Thomas Lewis now Lives) adjoyning to my said son Lawrence's Land above devised I also Give unto my said son Charles & his heirs the Land I purchased of Gabriel Adams in the County of Prince William Containing about seven hundred acres.

ITEM It is my will & desire that all the Rest of my Negroes not herein particularly Devised may be equally Divided between my wife and my three sons, Samuel, John and Charles & that, Ned, Jack, Bob, Sue & Lucy may be Included in my wifes part, which part of my said wife after her decease I Desire may be equally divided between my sons George, Samuel, John & Charles and the part of my said Negro's so devised to my wife‡ I mean & Intend to be in full satisfaction & Lieu of her Dower in my Negro's. But if she should insist

---

* John Augustine Washington, married Hannah Bushrod.
† Married Mildred Thornton.
‡ Mary Ball.

notwithstanding

notwithstanding on her Right of Dower in my Negro's I will & desire that so many as may be wanting to make up her share may be taken out of the Negro's given hereby to my sons George, Sam!. John and Charles.

ITEM I Give and Bequeath unto my said wife and my four sons, George, Samuel, John and Charles all the rest of my personal Estate to be equally Divided between them which is not particularly by this my will. And it is my Will and desire that my said four son's Estates may be kept in my wife's hand untill they respectively attain the Age of Twenty one years in Case my wife Continues so long unmarried, but in Case she should happen to marry before that time, I Desire it may be in the power of my Executors to oblige her husband from time to time as they shall think proper to give Security for the performance of this my Last Will in paying and Delivering my four sons their Estates respectively as they Come of age, or on failure to give such Security to take my said Sons & their Estates out of the Custody & Tuition of my said wife and her Husband.

ITEM I Give and bequeath unto my said wife the Crops made at Bridge Creek, Chotank and Rappahannock Quarters at the time of my Decease for the support of herself and her Children and I desire my wife may have the Liberty of working my Land at Bridge Creek Quarter for the term of
Five

Five Years next after my Decease during which time she may fix a Quarter on Deep Run.*

ITEM I give to my son Lawrence Washington and the heirs of his Body Lawfully begotten that Tract of Land I purchased of Mr. James Nore adjoining to the said Law. Washington's Land on Mattox in the County of Westmoreland which I Gave him in Lieu of the Land my said son bought for me in prince William County of Spencer & Harrison and ·for want of such heirs I give and devise the same to my son Augustine and his heirs forever. †

ITEM I give to my said son Lawrence all the right Title and Interest I have to in or out of the Iron works in which I am Concerned in Virginia & Maryland provided that he do and shall out of the profits raised thereby purchase for my said Augustine three Young Working Slaves as I have hereinbefore directed, and also paying my Daughter Betty when she arrives to the age of eighteen years the sum of four hundred pounds, which Right Title & Interest on the Condition aforesaid

---

* *Post.*

† By a lease dated 30 July, 1708, Francis Spencer leased to William Harrison, 200 acres of land on Dogue River. William Spencer in 1739 gave a release to Lawrence Washington for 200 acres of land in Prince William County; and in 1739 a similar release was given for land in the same county by George Harrison.

I give

I give to my said son Lawrence and his heirs forever.*

---

* These shares were in the Principio company, composed of English ironmasters and capitalists, which opened works in Maryland in 1715, and existed for more than sixty years. After establishing the Maryland works, the company were negotiating the purchase of some of Augustine Washington's land in Virginia; and in 1725 a furnace at Accokeek, in King George County, fourteen miles from Fredericksburg, was located. Augustine's connection with the company probably dates from this purchase, and he doubtless received a share in the undertaking, a contract for raising the ore and carting it to the furnace, and probably a bonus mentioned in the following letter: "As to ye deviding ye shares of ye new founded works in Virginia, have advised with a Counselor about it . . . who tells me y! except some persons here is appointed y? lawful aturney, by a power of atturney from you to signe for you here, y^t if your deed or deeds come over for you to signe in England and either of you should dy before, or alter your minds y! you dont sign, than it setts Washington at liberty and all ye work is at an end. . . . But think a twelfth too small for myselfe in this concerne . . . If you see fitt to make Capt. Washington a small present of wine (along ye Virginia Cargo) and to signifie to him y! what I have done with him on ye behalfe you like and approve on, or to that effect, y! I leave to your Consideration either to do it or not." *Letter of John England*, 5 January, 1725. Some twenty-five years after (1753) the supply of ore at Accokeek failed, "the movable effects were distributed among the other works, slaves and store-goods, horses, cattle, and wagons were sold, and the business in Virginia, as far as related to iron-making, was gradually closed up, some of the real estate being sold in 1767." At the death of Augustine, his share went to Lawrence, who also appears to have occupied a prominent position in its affairs, for he signed on behalf of the company the important purchase of the Lancashire furnace (1751).

Item

ITEM I give unto my said Daughter Betty a Negro Child named Mary Daughter of Sue, & another named Betty Daughter of Judy.

ITEM it is my will & desire that my sons Lawrence and Augustine do pay out of the respective Estates devised to them one half or moiety of the Debts I Justly owe and for that purpose I give and Bequeath unto my said Two sons one half of the Debts due & owing to me.

ITEM Forasmuch as my several Children in this my will mentioned being by several Ventures cannot inherit from one another in order to make a proper Provision ag^t their dying without Issue. It is my will and desire that in Case my son Lawrence should dye without heirs of his body Lawfully begotten that then the Land and Mill given him by this my Will lying in the County of Prince William shall go & remain to my son George & his heirs, but in Case my son Augustine should Choose to have the said Lands Rather than the Lands he holds in Maddox either by this will or any settle-

---

England's letter indicated a division of the company's capital into twelve shares, and Augustine must have received one undivided share. In 1780, when the property of the company had been confiscated as British possession, it was represented that a "certain Mr. Washington, a subject of the State of Virginia, is entitled to one undivided twelfth part thereof"—showing the share still intact. These facts are given in a series of articles by Mr. Henry Whitely, on the Principio Company, printed in the *Pennsylvania Magazine of History and Biography*, 1887.

ment

ment Then I give & devise the said Lands in Prince William to my said Son Augustine and his heirs, on his Conveying the said Lands in Maddox to my said son George and his heirs And in Case my said son Augustine shall happen to die without Issue of his Body Lawfully begotten Then I give and bequeath all the said Lands by him held in Maddox to my said son George and his heirs. And if both my sons Lawrence and Augustine should happen to die without Issue of their several Body's begotten Then my will & desire is that my son George and his heirs may have his and their Choice either to have the Lands of my son Lawrence or the Lands of my son Augustine to hold to him and his heirs and the Land of such of my said sons Lawrence or Augustine as shall not be so Chosen by my son George or his heirs shall go to and be equally Divided among my sons Samuel John & Charles and their heirs share and share alike and in Case my son George by the death of both or either of my sons Lawrence & Augustine should according to this my Intention come to be possessed of either of the Lands then my will & desire is that ye Land hereby devised to my said son George and his heirs should Go over and be equally divided between my sons Samuel & John and their heirs share and share alike. And in Case all my children by my present wife should happen to die without Issue of their Body's Then my will and desire is that all the
Lands

Lands by this my will devised to any of my said Children should go to my sons Augustine & Lawrence if Living & to their heirs or if one of them should be dead without Issue then to the Survivor & his heirs. but my true Intent and meaning is that each of my Children by my present wife may have their Lands in fee simple upon the Contingency, of their arriving at full age or Leaving heirs of their Body's Lawfully begotten or on their daying under age and without Lawfull Issue their several parts to descend from one to another according to their Course of descents, and the Remainder over of their or any of their Land in the Clause mentioned to my sons Lawrence & Augustine or the Survivor of them is only upon the Contingency of all my said Children by my present wife dying under age or without Issue Living my sons Lawrence and Augustine or either of them.

LASTLY I Constitute and appoint my son Lawrence Washington and my good Friends Daniel McCarty and Nathaniel Chapman, Gent. Executors of this my Last Will and Testament. In witness whereof I have hereunto set my hand & Seal the Eleventh day of April 1743.

AUGUS. WASHINGTON. [SEAL.]

Signed sealed and Published
In the presence of us
   ROB: JACKSON,
   ANTHONY STROTHER,
   JAS. THOMSON.

Provided

Provided further that if my Lands at Chotank devised to my son Samuel should by Course of Law be taken away then I give to the said Samuel in Lieu thereof a Tract of Land in Westmoreland County where Benj^a Weeks and Thomas Finch now lives by estimation seven hundred acres. ITEM I bequeath to my son George One Lot of Land in the Town of Fredericksburgh which I purchased of Col^o John Waller also two other Lots in the said Town which I purchased of the Executors of Col^o Henry Willis with all the houses and Appurtenances thereunto belonging.* AND whereas some proposals have been made by Mr Anthony Strother for purchasing a piece of Land where Mathew Tiffy Lately liv'd now if my Executors shall think it for the Benefit of my son George then I hereby empower them to make a Conveyance of the said Land and Premises to the said Strother. IN WITNESS whereof I have hereunto set my hand and seale the eleventh day of April 1743.

AUGUS. WASHINGTON. [SEAL.]

Signed sealed and Published
In the presence of us
  ROB: JACKSON,
  ANTHONY STROTHER,
  JA^s THOMSON.

---

* "Deeds for Lots in the town of Fredericksburg, of no Value to the Subscriber being sold by the Ex'r of his Father, for his benefit, and the hands into which they are got unknown to G. Washington." *MS. memorandum of Washington.*

At a

At a Court held for King George County the 6° day of May 1743.

The Last Will and Testament of Augustine Washington Gent was presented into Court by Lawrence Washington one of his Executors who made Oath thereto and the same was proved by the Oath of Anthony Strother and James Thompson and admitted to Record.

Cop^e. Test

HARRY TURNER,

Cl. Cur.*

---

* "Wakefield," on Pope's Creek, was devised by the immigrant John to his son, Lawrence, from whom it passed at his death to his wife, and then to his son John. It is said that this John sold the tract to his brother Augustine, the father of George, and was left by him to his son, Augustine, a half-brother of George. Augustine left it, with other property in Westmoreland County, to his son William Augustine, and the latter gave it to his son, George Corbin Washington, who sold it to John Gray, reserving a space of sixty feet square around the site of the house, where George Washington was born, and another of twenty feet square around the burial ground and vault of the Washington family. Lewis William, a son and heir at law of George Corbin Washington, ceded these reservations to "the mother state of Virginia, in perpetuity, on condition solely that the State require the said places to be permanently enclosed with an iron fence based on stone foundations, together with suitable and modest (though substantial) tablets, to commemorate to the rising generation these notable spots." The grant was accepted and $5,000 appropriated to make good the conditions on which the grant was made.

In 1815 George Washington Parke Custis had with theatrical

effects placed a slab of freestone to mark the birthplace, bearing this inscription:

Here
the 11th of February, 1732
George Washington
was born.

Before 1860 this slab had broken into three pieces.

EDM.ᴰ PENDLETON TO GEORGE WASHINGTON.

3ᵈ July 1769.

Dr. Sir

I have at last found leizure to peruse & consider the papers you left with me for my opinion on the nature of your Interest in your Fairfax Lands.*

The deed of Settlement made by your Father on your brother Lawrence is long & complicated occasioned chiefly by an Intention to provide against the contingencie of the Prince Wᵐ Lands which were the subject of that deed & the Westmorland Lands Formerly settled upon Augustine, from coming into the same hands by the death of one of your brothers without Issue, but as I take it for granted that your brother Augᵗ chose to keep the Westmorlᵈ Lands, and not to

---

* Ann, the widow of Lawrence Washington, married George Lee, of Westmoreland. Her life interest in Mount Vernon and the slaves, with a grist mill, was made over to George Washington by a deed, recorded 17 December, 1754, in consideration of an annual payment of fifteen thousand pounds of tobacco in fifteen hogsheads, to be delivered at the warehouses in Fairfax county, or 12 shillings six pence, current money, for every hundred weight of tobacco. The average annual sum paid under this agreement was £87. On her death, the Mount Vernon estate became the property of George, but by the terms of Lawrence's will, he had only a life estate. It was this provision of Lawrence's will that led George to consult Pendleton upon his right to dispose of the Mt. Vernon lands.

An opinion by Judge Bushrod Washington was sold at the Philadelphia sale, but I am unable to trace its possession.

give them up & take to the Prince William Lands as he had power to do upon the death of Lawrence without Issue, great part of that settlement is of little consequence, as to the Point you now want to be satisfied in.

The Prince William Lands then are limited to Lawrence in fee simple upon the Contingencie of his *leaving Issue at his death.* He takes Notice of a daughter* in his will & if she survived him, your fathers Will has no operation upon the estate, but it must go according to the Will of y:r brother Lawrence by which you take an estate tail, with a remainder to your brother Aug:t in fee simple; for tho' the words of the devising clause would give you a fee, yet by a Subsequent one he directs that if you, Sam:l John & Charles or any of you, *die without Lawful Issue* such Land as was given you or any of you, should become the property of his brother Augustine & his heirs forever, which changes your and their Estates in all the Lands Claimed under his will, into estates tail.

If indeed the daughter of Lawrence died before him, then as he left no Issue, the Land by the settlement was to be subject to your fathers disposition and by his Will you have a fee simple in the Prince William Lands, under the Remainder limited to you if Law. died without Issue, since one of the contingencies upon w:ch you were to have a fee, has happened, that of your arriving to full age, Altho' you have no Issue. If this latter was the case, and you would choose to support y:r fee simple, it might be proper to bring a Bill in

---

* Sarah.

Chancery

Chancery to Perpetuate testimony to prove the fact of her dying before her father, as without testimony the presumption would be that she survived, being named in his Will; Nothing Further Occurs to me necessary to be mentioned. I am, Sir,

     Your Mo. Ob^{t} hble Servt
       EDM^D PENDLETON.

WILL

OF

MARY (BALL) WASHINGTON,

MOTHER OF

GEORGE WASHINGTON.

In the Name of God! amen—I Mary Washington of Fredericksg in the County of Spotsylvania, being in good health, but calling to mind the uncertainty of this Life and willing to dispose of what remains of my worldly Estate, do make & publish this my last will, recommending my Soul into the Hands of my Creator, hoping for a remission of all my sins through the merits & mediation of JESUS CHRIST, the saveour of Mankind; I dispose of all my worldly Estate as follows—

IMPRIMIS I give to my Son General George Washington all my lands on Accokeek Run in the County of Stafford & also my Negroe Boy George to him and his Heirs forever. & also my best bed, beadstead of Virginia Cloth Curtains (the same that stands in my best Room) my quilted blue & white Quilt & my best dressing Glass—

ITEM I give and devise to my son Charles Washington my negroe Man Tom to him & his assigns for ever.

ITEM I give and devise to my Daughter Betty Lewis my Phæton & my bay Horse

ITEM I give & devise to my Daughter in Law Hannah Washington my purple Cloath cloak lined with Shag.

ITEM I give & devise to my grandson Corbin Washington

Washington my Negroe wench Old Bet my riding Chair & two blk Horses, to him and his assigns for ever.

ITEM I give and devise to my grandson Fielding Lewis my Negroe man Frederick to him & his assigns for ever, also eight silver tablespoons, half my crokery ware, of the blue & white Tea * * * book case, table, my Bed bedstead, one p^r sheets, one p^r. blankets & white cotton counterpaine, two table cloaths, six red leather chairs, half my pewter & one half of my Iron kitchen Furniture—

ITEM I give and devise to my grandson Lawrence Lewis my negro wench Lydia to him and his assigns for ever.

ITEM I give and devise to my grand daughter Betty Carter my negro woman little Bet & her future increase to her and her assigns for ever— also my largest looking glass, my walnut writing Desk with Drawers, a square dining Table, one Bed, Bedstead, bolster, one pillow, one blanket & p^r. sheets, white Virginia cloth Counterpane & purple Curtains, my red and white tea China, spoons, & the other half of my pewter, crokery ware, & the remainder of my Iron kitchen Furniture.

ITEM I give to my grand Son George Washington my next best best dressing Glass one Bead, Bedstead bolster, 1 pillow, 1 p^r. sheet, Blanket & counterpaine.

ITEM

ITEM I devise all my wearing apparel to be equally divided between my grand Daughters, Betty Carter, Fanny Ball, & Milly Washington—but shou'd my Daughter Betty Lewis fancy any one two or three articles, she is to have them before a division thereof—

LASTLY I nominate & appoint my said son General George Washington Executor of this my will. And as I owe few or no debts, I direct my Executor to give no security, nor to appraise my Estate, but desire the same may be allotted to my Devisees with as little trouble & delay as may be—desiring their acceptance thereof as a little Token I now have to give them of my love for them. In witness whereof I have hereunto set my Hand and seal this 20th day of May 1788.

MARY WASHINGTON.

Signed sealed and published in our presence & signed by us in the presence of the s^d Mary Washington & at her desire.

J^s MERCER
JOSEPH WALKER

At a Court of Hustings held for the town & Corporation of Fredericksburg the 23^d day of October 1789.

The last Will and Testament of Mary Washington Dec^d was proved by the Oath of James Mercer, Esq.

Esq. one of the Witnesses thereto and Ordered to be certified.

Teste

JN? CHEW, C. C. H.

At a Court of Hustings held for the Town & Corporation of Fredericksburg the 22ᵈ day of October 1804

The last will & testament of Mary Washington, decᵈ was further proved by the Oath of Joseph Walker, another Witness thereto and ordered to be Recorded.

Teste

JN? CHEW, C. C. H.*

---

* This will was reproduced in *fac-simile* and printed in the *Magazine of American History*, March, 1887, in one of Mr. Conway's articles on Fredericksburg.

Joseph Ball had left to his sister "400 acres of land in Richmond county, in yᵉ freshes of Rappahn. River." This property she conveyed 21 May, 1778, to John Augustine Washington, and the land was described as lying near Fredericksburg. Her husband had given her the privilege of working his land at the Bridge Creek quarter for five years after his decease, "during which time she may fix a quarter on Deep Run;" but the land on Deep Run was divided between George and Samuel. "As my mother's term of years is out at the place at Bridge Creek, she designs to settle a quarter on the piece at Deep Run, but seems backward in doing it till the right is made good for fear of accident." *George Washington to Lawrence Washington*, 5 May, 1749. On Fry and Jefferson's map Deep Run is placed about seven miles above Falmouth, and Deep Creek is down by "Moratico," the Joseph Ball place, the distance between the

GEORGE WASHINGTON TO MRS. BETTY LEWIS.

NEW YORK, 13 September, 1789.

My dear Sister,

Colonel Ball's* letter gave me the first account of my mother's death.† Since that I have received Mrs. Carter's letter, written at your request, and previous to both I was prepared for the event by some advices of her illness communicated to your son Robert.

Awful and affecting as the death of a parent is, there is consolation in knowing, that heaven has spared ours to an age beyond which few attain, and favored her with the full enjoyment of her mental faculties, and as much bodily strength as usually falls to the lot of four score. Under these considerations, and a hope that she is translated to a happier place, it is the duty of her relatives to yield due submission to the decrees of the Creator. When I was last at Fredericksburg, I took a final leave of my mother, never expecting to see her more.

It will be impossible for me at this distance, and circumstanced as I am, to give the smallest attention to the execution of her will; nor indeed is much required,

---

two being more than fifty miles. It is probable that Deep Run was the place, and that Mrs. Washington did remove there and set up a quarter, as Washington visits her in passing from Dumfries to Fredericksburg.

*Burges Ball.

†Mary Washington died at Fredericksburg, August 25th, 1789, in the eighty-third year of her age. She had been a widow forty-six years. General Washington's father died on the 12th of April, 1743.

if,

if, as she directs, no security should be given, or appraisement made of her estate; but that the same should be allotted to the devisees with as little trouble and delay as may be. How far this is legal, I know not. Mr. Mercer can, and I have no doubt would, readily advise you if asked, which I wish you to do. If the ceremony of inventorying, appraising, &c. can be dispensed with, all the rest, (as the will declares that|few or no debts are owing,) can be done with very little trouble. Every person may in that case immediately receive what is specifically devised. The negroes who are engaged in the crops and under an overseer, must remain I conceive on the plantation until the crop is finished (which ought to be as soon as possible) after which the horses, stock of all sorts, and every species of property not disposed of by the will, (the debts if any being first paid) must by law be equally divided into five parts one of which you, another my Brother Charles and a third myself are entitled to, the other two thirds fall to the share of the children of our deceased brothers Samuel and John.

Were it not, that the specific legacies, which are given to me by the will, are meant and ought to be considered and received as mementos of parental affection, in the last solemn act of life, I should not be desirous of receiving or removing them; but in this point of view I set a value on them much beyond their intrinsic worth.

Whilst it occurs to me, it is necessary it should be known that there is a fellow belonging to that estate now at my house, who never stayed elsewhere, for which

which reason, and because he has a family I should be glad to keep him. He must I should conceive be far short in value of the fifth of the other negroes which will be to be divided, but I shall be content to take him as my proportion of them—and, if from a misconception either of the number or the value of these negroes it should be found that he is of greater value than falls to my lot I shall readily allow the difference, in order that the fellow may be gratified, as he never would consent to go from me.

Debts, if any are due, should be paid from the sale of the crops, Plantation utensils, Horses and Stock, and the sooner an account is taken of the latter and they can conveniently be disposed of, the better it will be for two reasons; first because the Overseer (if he is not a very honest man) may take advantage of circumstances, and convert part of these things to his own use —and secondly because the Season is now fast approaching when without feeding (which would lessen the sale of the corn and fodder) the stock will fall off, and consequently sell to a disadvantage. Whether my Mother has kept any accounts that can be understood is more than I am able to say—If any thing is owing to her it should be received—and, if due from her, paid after due proof thereof is made—She has had a great deal of money from me at times, as can be made appear by my books, and the accounts of Mr. L. Washington during my absence;—and over and above this has not only had all that was ever made from the Plantation but got her provisions and every thing else she thought proper from thence. In short to the best of my recollection

lection I have never in my life received a copper from the estate—and have paid many hundred pounds (first and last) to her in cash—However I want no retribution—I conceived it to be a duty whenever she asked for money, and I had it, to furnish her, notwithstanding she got all the crops or the amount of them and took every thing she wanted from the plantation for the support of her family, horses &c. besides.

As the accounts for or against the estate must not only from the declaration in the will, but from the nature of the case be very trifling and confined I should suppose to the town of Fredericksburg, it might be proper therefore in that paper to require in an advertisement all those who have any demands to bring them in properly attested immediately, and those who are owing to pay forthwith. The same advertisement might appoint a day for selling the stock, and every thing, excepting Negroes, at the plantation, that is not devised by the will, as it will be more convenient I should suppose for the heirs to receive their respective dividends of the money arising from the sales than to be troubled with receiving a cow, a calf, or such like things after the debts (which must be the case) have been first paid. It might be well in fixing the day of sale, to consult the Overseer, to know when the business of the plantation will admit the Cart, Team and Utensils to be taken from it.

As the number of articles to be sold cannot be many and will be of small value, I think they had better be sold for ready money and so advertised, for though they would fetch more on credit, there would more
than

than probable be bad debts contracted, and at any rate delay, if not law suits before the money could be collected, and besides if there are debts to be paid money will be wanted for the purpose, and in no way can be so readily and properly obtained as by a ready money sale, and from the crops.

If you think this business will be too troublesome for you with the aid of your sons—Mr. Carter and Colonel Ball—who I am persuaded will give each of us assistance, and you will let me know it, I will desire Major George Washington to attend.

As the land at the Little-falls Plantation goes to Mr. Bushrod Washington he should be apprised in time of the breaking of it up, otherwise there may be injury to the houses and fencing if left without some person to attend to them. Have particular care taken of her papers, the letters to her, &c.

I should prefer selling the houses and lotts on which my Mother lived to renting of them,—and would give a year or two years' credit to the purchasers paying interest—and not being acquainted with the value of lotts in Fredericksburg, I would leave the price to any three indifferent and impartial Gentleman to say what they are worth, and that sum I will take.

If they cannot be sold and soon, I would rent them from year to year to any orderly Tenant on a moderate rent. If they are not disposed of on sale or by tennanting before the weather gets cool the paling will, I expect, be soon burnt up.

Give my love to Mrs. Carter, and thank her for the letter she wrote to me. I would have done this myself,

self, had I more time for private correspondences. Mrs. Washington joins in best wishes for her, yourself, and all other friends; and I am, with the most sincere regard, your affectionate brother.

GEORGE WASHINGTON TO MRS. BETTY LEWIS.

NEW YORK, 12 October, 1789.

My dear Sister,

Your letter of the first of this month came duly to hand.—I believe Bushrod is right with respect to the distribution of the negroes—When I gave my opinion that you were entitled to a child's part it did not occur to me that my Mother held them under the will of my Father who had made a distribution of them after her death.—If this is the case, and I believe it is, you do not come in for any part of them.

I thought I had desired in my former letter that all personal property not specifically disposed of by the will had better be sold. This is my opinion, as it is from the crops and personal Estate that the Debts must be paid.—The surplus, be it more or less, is divided among her children; and this I presume had better be done in money than in Stock, old furniture or any other troublesome articles which might be inconvenient to remove, but in one or the other of these ways they must be disposed of, as they are not given by the Will.—If there is anything coming to the Estate it ought to be collected.—In a word, all the property except Lands and negroes is considered as personal, and after the Debts are discharged is to be equally

equally divided into five parts, one of which you are entitled to. * * *

G? WASHINGTON.*

GEORGE WASHINGTON TO COL. BURGES BALL AND CHARLES CARTER, JR.

NEW HAVEN, 18 October, 1789.

Dear Sirs,

Having set out on a tour through the Eastern States, it was at this place your letter of the 8th inst. overtook me.

Not having my father's will to recur to, when I wrote to my sister, nor any recollection of the Devises in it, I supposed she was entitled to a child's part of the Negroes, but, if they were otherwise disposed of by that Will (as I believe is the case) she is certainly excluded, and the sons only and their representatives come in. In this manner the division must be made.

Everything of personal property not specifically disposed of by my Mother's Will, had better be sold—with the proceeds of which, and the crops, the Debts must be paid. The surplus, if any, must be divided among the heirs.

Being well convinced that the Gentlemen who were so obliging as to examine and set a Value upon my Lots [in Fredericksburg], acted from their best judgment, I am perfectly satisfied with their decision, and beg my thanks may be presented to them for the trouble they have had in this business.

---

* From *George Washington & Mount Vernon*, lv.

If they are not already sold, I am willing to allow three, instead of two years credit for the payment of the purchase money, Interest being paid. In a word, as I do not tenant them, I should be glad to sell them on *any reasonable terms:* as that kind of property, at a distance, is always troublesome, and rarely productive.

I did not mean to give Mr Mercer the trouble of stating any formal opinion—All I had in view was to know if the formalities of the law, with respect to inventorying, appraising, &c., could be dispensed with.— If it could, I was sure no other difficulty would arise, as I knew my Mother's dealings were small, and the business consequently easily closed. * * *

G^o WASHINGTON.*

---

*From a transcript in the Department of State. The original is in the possession of Capt. Geo. Washington Ball, of Washington, D. C., to whose courtesy I am indebted for many favors.

THE WILL OF LAWRENCE WASHINGTON,

HALF-BROTHER OF GEORGE WASHINGTON.

IN THE NAME OF GOD AMEN, I Lawrence Washington of Truro parish, in Fairfax County, and Colony of Virginia, Gent.—knowing the uncertainty of this transitory life, and being in sound and disposing mind and memory do make this my last Will and Testament, hereby revoking and disannulling all other Wills and Testaments by me at any time heretofore made. IMPRIMIS, my will and desire is, that a proper vault, for interment, may be made on my home plantation, Wherein my remains together with my three children may be decently placed; and to serve for my wife, and such other of the family as may desire it.

ITEM, my Will and desire is that my Funeral charges and respective debts be first paid and discharged, out of such of my personal estate as my Executors hereafter to be named shall think best and most adviseable to be disposed of for that purpose. ITEM, my will and desire is that my loving Wife,* have the use benefits and profits of all my Lands on Little Hunting and Doegs Creeks, in the County of Truro and County of Fairfax with all the Houses and Edifices thereon, during her natural life, likewise the use, labour, and profits arising from the one half of all my Negroes, as my said wife and

---

*Anna Fairfax.   Executors

Executors may agree in dividing them. Negro Moll and her issue, to be included in my wife's part of the said Negroes. I also divise that my said wife may have the use of the Lands surveyed on the south fork of Bullskin, in the County of Frederick; during her natural Life, but in case of my daughter Sarah dying without issue before her said Mother, then I give and devize my said Bullskin Tract, to my said Wife; to her and her Heirs forever. ITEM, it is my Will and desire that all my Household Goods and furniture with the liquors to be appraised and valued by three persons to be chosen by my wife and Executors, and that my wife have the liberty of chooseing any part of the said Household goods and furniture to the amount of a full moiety of the whole sum, which they shall be appraised to, which part I give and bequeath to her and her Heirs forever; the other moiety to be sold, and the money arising applied towards the payment of my Debts.

ITEM, What I have herein devised and left to my Wife I intend to be in Lieu, and in stead, of her right of Dower, provided my Wife, according to her promise, sells her several Tracts of Land near Salisbury plains, and applys the said money to the discharge of my Debts due at the time of my Death, but in case of her refusal then my will is that all my Household furniture be sold, and the whole amount to be applied towards the discharge of of my Debts. ITEM I give and bequeath to my Daughter Sarah and the Heirs of her body, lawfully begotten forever, after my Just debts are discharged, all my real and personal Estate in Virginia, and the province of Maryland not otherwise disposed of. But in case it should please God my said Daughter, should die without issue, it is then my will and desire my Estate both real and personal be disposed of in the following manner;

First, I give and bequeath to my loveing Brother Augustine Washington and his Heirs forever, all my Stock, Interest and Estate in the Principio, Accokeek, Kingsbury, Lancashire, and N? East Iron Works in Virginia and Maryland, reserving one-third of the profits of said works, to be paid to my Wife, as hereafter mentioned, and Two Tracts of Land, lying and being in Frederick County which I purchased of Col? Cresap and Gerrard Pendergrass. Second, I give and bequeath unto my loving brother George Washington, and his Heirs forever, after the decease of my wife, all my lands in Fairfax County, with the improvements thereon and further it is my will and desire that during the natural life of my wife, that my said Brother George shall have the use of an equal Share, and proportion of all the Lands hereafter given and devised unto my brothers Samuel, John and Charles. Third, I give and bequeath all those several Tracts of Lands which I am possessed of
and

and claim in the County of Frederick (except the Tract on the south fork of Bull skin, bequeathed to my Wife, and the two Tracts purchased of Col° Cresap and Gerrard Pendergrass, devised unto my Brother Augustine) unto my Brothers Samuel, John and Charles, reserving as above an equal proportion for my Brother George, provided they, Samuel, John or Charles, pay or cause to be paid unto my and their sister Betty Lewis, the sum of One hundred and fifty pounds. Fourth, my Will also is that upon the death of any, or all of my said Brothers, George, Samuel, John and Charles, dying without lawful issue, such Lands as was given them or any of them, in case of my said Daughters demise as aforesaid, to become the property and Right of my Brother Augustine and his Heirs. Fifth, my further will and desire is, that after the demise of my said wife the Negro Woman, Moll and her increase be given unto my said Brother Augustine, his Heirs, adm'ors &c and likewise give him an equal proportion with his other Brothers, of the other part of the Negroes, and personal Estate, upon their paying my said Wife One hundred pounds Sterling my intent and meaning is that the said one hundred pounds sterling be paid by my said Brothers to my said wife immediately, or soon after, it may please God to remove by death my said Daughter.

ITEM, I further give and bequeath unto my loveing

ing wife, during her natural life one full third part of the profits from the share I hold in all the several Iron Works, both in the Colony of Virginia and Maryland, to be paid unto my said Wife from time to time by my Executors, immediately upon notice given them by the partners, residing in England, of the annual amount of the profits, to be paid either in Bills or Cash, at the current Exchange, as she shall choose.

ITEM, I give unto my brother John Washington, Fifty pounds in lieu of the Land taken from him by a suit at Law by Capt. Maxin.^r Robinson, after my debts are paid. ITEM, my will and desire is that my two Tracts of Land, one Joining my wife's Tract, near Salisbury plain, the other on a branch of Goose Creek, being three Hundred and three Acres, my Two Lots in the Town of Alexandria with the edifices thereon, and my share and Interest in the Ohio Company, all be sold by my Executors, and the money applied towards discharging my debts, also my arrears of half pay, which Col^o Wilson, the agent, or Mr Stuart, his Kinsman and Clerk, be addressed for and the money applied to the same use. ITEM, whereas the purchasing Negroes and Land may greatly tend to the advantage of my Daughter, I therefore fully empower my Executors to lay out the profit of my Estate, or any part thereof in Lands, and Negroes at their discretion, i. e. I mean such

such part of the Estate as I have devised to my Daughter Sarah, which said several purchases, in case of her decease without Issue, shall be deemed and counted personal Estate, and be accordingly equally divided among my Brothers as above provided.

ITEM I also desire that my Just suit of complaint at Law, depending against Gersham Keys, of Frederick county, for breach of Trust, be effectually prosecuted by my Executors.

ITEM, it is furthermore my will and desire that all my Estate be kept together till the debts are discharged.

ITEM I give to my wife, my Mother in Law, and each of my Executors, a mourning ring;

LASTLY, I constitute and appoint the Honb! William Fairfax and George Fairfax, Esqr, my said Brothers, Augustine and George Washington, and my esteemed Friends, Mr Nathaniel Chapman and Maj^r John Carlyle, Executors of this my last will and Testament. Whereof I have hereunto set my Hand and Seale, this twentieth day of June, one Thousand Seven Hundred and fifty two, in the 26th year of his Majesty King George the second's Reign.

     LAW^E WASHINGTON   [SEAL].

Signed, sealed & published in the presence of us
 W^M WAITE,   J^{NO} NORTH,
   his   JOSEPH GOUND.
 ANDREW ✕ W. WARREN,
   mark

              At

At a Court held for Fairfax County September the 26th 1752, This Last Will and Testament of Lawrence Washington Gent. dece'd was presented in Court by the Honb'l. William Fairfax and George William Fairfax, Esq'r. John Carlyle and George Washington, Gent'n. four of the Executors therein named who made oath thereto according to Law, and being proved by the oaths of William Waite, John North and Andrew Warren, three of the Witnesses, is admitted to Record, and the said Executors, performing what is usual in such cases, certificate is granted them, for obtaining a probate in due form.

      Test.
         JOHN GRAHAM,
           Cl.

A true Copy
 Test
  W'm. Moss, Cl.

THE WILL

OF

GEORGE WASHINGTON.

IN THE NAME OF GOD, AMEN!

I GEORGE WASHINGTON of Mount Vernon, a citizen of the United States and lately President of the same do make ordain and declare this Instrument, which is written with my own hand and every page thereof subscribed with my name to be my last Will & Testament, revoking all others.*

—Imprimus—All my debts, of which there are but few, and none of magnitude, are to be punctually and speedily paid, and the legacies hereinafter bequeathed are to be discharged as soon as circumstances will permit, and in the manner directed.

ITEM. To my dearly beloved wife, Martha Washington I give and bequeath the use profit and benefit of my whole Estate, real and personal, for

---

*At the bottom of every page—with one exception—he signed his name. On the one page, the last word was Washington, which probably led him to suppose he had signed.

There is mention of an earlier will to be found in a letter written to his wife just after he had accepted the command of the Continental army. "As life is always uncertain, and common prudence dictates to every man the necessity of settling his temporal concerns, while it is in his power, and while the mind is calm and undisturbed, I have, since I came to this place (for I had not time to do it before I left home) got Colonel Pendleton to draft a will for me, by the directions I gave him, which will I now enclose. The provision made for you in case of my death will, I hope, be agreeable." 18 June, 1775.

the

the term of her natural life, except such parts thereof as are specially disposed of hereafter,—My improved lot in the Town of Alexandria, situated on Pitt and Cameron Streets, I give to her & her heirs forever, as I also do my [2]* household and kitchen furniture of every sort and kind with the liquors and groceries which may be on hand at the time of my decease, to be used and disposed of as she may think proper.

ITEM—Upon the decease of wife it is my will and desire, that all the slaves which I hold in *my own right* shall receive their freedom—To emancipate them during her life, would tho earnestly wished by me, be attended with such insuperable difficulties, on account of their intermixture by marriages with the Dower negroes as to excite the most painful sensations—if not disagreeable consequences from the later while both descriptions are in the occupancy of the same proprietor, it not being in my power under the tenure by which the dower Negroes are held to manumit them—And whereas among those who will receive freedom according to this devise there may be some who from old age, or bodily infirmities & others who on account of their infancy, that will be unable to support themselves, it is my will and desire that all who come under the first and second description

---

* These figures in brackets mark the beginning of each page of the *MS.* will.

shall

shall be comfortably clothed and fed by my heirs while they live and [3] that such of the latter description as have no parents living, or if living are unable, or unwilling to provide for them, shall be bound by the Court until they shall arrive at the age of twenty five years, and in cases where no record can be produced whereby their ages can be ascertained, the Judgment of the Court upon it's own view of the subject shall be adequate and final.—The negroes thus bound are (by their masters or mistresses) to be taught to read and write and to be brought up to some useful occupation, agreeably to the laws of the commonwealth of Virginia, providing for the support of orphans and other poor children—and I do hereby expressly forbid the sale or transportation out of the said Commonwealth of any Slave I may die possessed of, under any pretence, whatsoever—and I do moreover most positively, and most solemnly enjoin it upon my Executors hereafter named, or the survivors of them to see that this clause respecting slaves and every part thereof be religiously fulfilled at the Epoch at which it is directed to take place without evasion neglect or delay after the crops which may then be on the ground are harvested, particularly as it respects [4] the aged and infirm, seeing that a regular and permanent fund be established for their support so long as there are subjects requiring it, not trusting to the uncertain provisions

ions to be made by individuals.—And to my mulatto man, William (calling himself William Lee) I give immediate freedom or if he should prefer it (on account of the accidents which have befallen him and which have rendered him incapable of walking or of any active employment*) to remain in the situation he now is, it shall be optional in him to do so —In either case however I allow him an annuity of thirty dollars during his natural life which shall be independent of the victuals and *cloaths* he has been accustomed to receive; if he *chuses* the last alternative, but in full with his freedom, if he prefers the first, and this I give him as a testimony of my sense of his attachment to me and for his faithful services during the revolutionary War.†

---

*On 22d April, 1785, when acting as chain bearer, while Washington was surveying a tract of land on Four Mile Run, William fell, and broke his knee pan; "which put a stop to my surveying; and with much difficulty I was able to get him to Abingdon, being obliged to get a sled to carry him on, as he could neither walk, stand or ride." *Washington's Diary.* See *Spurious Letters attributed to Washington*, 8.

† The following letters relate to this servant:

GEORGE WASHINGTON TO CLEMENT BIDDLE.

MOUNT VERNON, 28 July, 1784.

Dear Sir,

The mulatto fellow, William, who has been with me all the war, is attached (married he says) to one of his own color, a free woman, who during the war, was also of my family. She has been in an infirm condition for some time, and I had conceived

ITEM

ITEM—To the Trustees, (Governors or by whatsoever other name they may be designated) of the academy in the Town of Alexandria, I give and bequeath, in Trust, Four thousand dollars, or in other words twenty of the shares which I [5] hold

that the connexion between them had ceased; but I am mistaken it seems they are both applying to get her here, and tho' I never wished to see her more, I cannot refuse his request (if it can be complied with on reasonable terms) as he has served me faithfully for many years.

After premising thus much, I have to beg the favor of you to procure her a passage to Alexanda., either by Sea, in the Stage, or in the passage boat from the head of Elk, as you shall think cheapest and best, and her situation will admit;—the cost of either I will pay. Her name is Margaret Thomas allias Lee (the name by which *he* calls himself). She lives in Philada. with Isaac and Hannah Sile—black people, who are often employ'd by families in the city as cooks.

I am &c.

TOBIAS LEAR TO COLO. CLEMENT BIDDLE.

NEW YORK, 3 May, 1789.

Dear Sir,

Your letter of the 27th ulto. came duly to the hands of the President. He would thank you to propose it to Will to return to Mount Vernon when he can be removed for he cannot be of any service here, and perhaps will require a person to attend upon him constantly. If he should incline to return to Mount Vernon, you will be so kind as to have him sent in the first Vessel that sails for Alexandria after he can be removed with safety—but if he is still anxious to come on here the President would gratify him Altho' he will be troublesome—He has been an old and faithful Servant this is enough for the President to gratify him in every reasonable wish— * * *

I am &c.   TOBIAS LEAR.

in the Bank of Alexandria towards the support of a Free School, established at, and annexed to the said academy for the purpose of educating such orphan children, or the children of such other poor and indigent persons as are unable to accomplish it with their own means, and who in the judgment of the trustees of the said Seminary, are best entitled to the benefit of this donation—The aforesaid twenty shares I give and bequeath in perpetuity—the dividends only of which are to be drawn for and applied by the said Trustees for the time being, for the uses above mentioned, the stock to remain entire and untouched unless indications of a failure of the said Bank should be so apparent or discontinuance thereof should render a removal of this fund necessary, in either of these cases the amount of the stock here devised is to be vested in some other bank or public institution whereby the interest may with regularity and certainty be drawn and applied as above.—And to prevent misconception, my meaning is, and is hereby declared to be that, these twenty shares are in lieu of and not in addition to the Thousand pounds given by a missive letter some years ago in consequence whereof an an[6]nuity of fifty pounds has since been paid towards the support of this institution.*

---

*This letter is printed in Washington's Writings (Ford's edition), xi., —.

In his MS. *Diary* for 1785 is found the following entry under
ITEM

ITEM—Whereas by a law of the Commonwealth of Virginia, enacted in the year 1785, the Legislature thereof was pleased (as an evidence of it's approbation of the services I had rendered the public, during the Revolution—and partly, I believe in consideration of my having suggested the vast advantages which the community would derive from the extension of its Inland navigation, under Legislative patronage) to present me with one hundred shares, of one hundred dollars each, in the incorporated company established for the purpose of extending the navigation of James River from tide water to the mountains; and also with fifty shares of one hundred pounds sterling each in the corporation of another company likewise established for the similar purpose of opening the navigation of the River Potomac from tide water to Fort Cumberland; the acceptance of which, although the offer was highly honorable and grateful to my feel-

---

date December 17th: "Went to Alexandria to meet the trustees of the Academy in that place, and offered to vest in the hands of the said Trustees, when they are permanently established by Charter, the sum of one thousand pounds, the interest of which only to be applied towards the establishment of a charity school for the education of Orphan and other poor children, which offer was accepted." His letter to the Trustees is printed in *Washington's Writings* (Sparks') ix., 151. The act of incorporation was passed by the Legislature in the October session, 1786, and Washington was named first in the list of trustees. *Hening's Statutes*, xii., 392.

ings,

ings, was refused, as inconsistent with a principle which I had adop[7]ted, and had never departed from, namely not to receive pecuniary compensation for any services I could render my country in it's arduous struggle with Great Britain for it's Rights; and because I had evaded similar propositions from other States in the Union—adding to this refusal however an intimation, that, if it should be the pleasure of the Legislature to permit me to appropriate the said shares to *public uses*, I would receive them on those terms with due sensibility—and this it having consented to in flattering terms, as will appear by a subsequent law and sundry resolutions, in the most ample and honorable manner,* I proceed after this recital for the more correct understanding of the case to declare—

That as it has always been a source of serious regret with me to see the youth of these United States sent to foreign countries for the purpose of education, often before their minds were formed or they had imbibed any adequate ideas of the happiness of their own, contracting too frequently not only habits of dissipation and *extravagence*, but principles unfriendly to Republican Governm't and to the true and genuine liberties [8] of mankind,

---

*The various laws may be found in Hening, *Statutes at Large*, xi., 543; xii., 42. The letters of Washington are in my xi.

which

which thereafter are rarely overcome.—For these reasons it has been my ardent wish to see a plan devised on a liberal scale which would have a tendency to spread systamatic ideas through all parts of this rising Empire, thereby to do away local attachments and state prejudices as far as the nature of things would, or indeed ought to admit, from our national councils—Looking anxiously forward to the accomplishment of so desirable an object as this is, (in my estimation) my mind has not been able to contemplate any plan more likely to effect the measure than the establishment of a University in a central part of the United States to which the youth of fortune and talents from all parts thereof might be sent for the completion of their education in all the branches of polite literature in arts and sciences—in acquiring knowledge in the principles of Politics and good Government and (as a matter of infinite importance in my judgment) by associating with each other and forming friendships in Juvenile years, be enabled to free themselves in a proper degree from those local prejudices and habit[9]ual jealousies which have just been mentioned and which when carried to excess are never failing sources of disquietude to the Public mind and pregnant of mischieveous consequences to this country:—under these impressions so fully dilated,—

ITEM—I give and bequeath in perpetuity the fifty

fifty shares which I hold in the Potomac Company (under the aforesaid Acts of the Legislature of Virginia) towards the endowment of a University to be established within the limits of the District of Columbia, under the auspices of the General Government, if that Government should incline to extend a fostering hand towards it,—and until such seminary is established, and the funds arising on these shares shall be required for its support, my further will and desire is that the profit accruing therefrom shall whenever the dividends are made be laid out in purchasing stock in the Bank of Columbia or some other Bank at the discretion of my Executors, or by the Treasurer of the United States for the time being under the direction of Congress, provided that Honorable body should [10] *patronize* the measure. And the dividends proceeding from the purchase of such Stock is to be vested in more Stock and so on until a sum adequate to the accomplishment of the object is obtained, of which I have not the smallest doubt before many years pass away, even if no aid or *encouraged* is given by Legislative authority or from any other source.*

ITEM—The hundred shares which I held in the James River Company I have given and now confirm in perpetuity to and for the use and benefit of

---

* This provision of the will was never carried into effect.

Liberty

Liberty Hall Academy in the County of Rockbridge, in the Commonwealth of *Virga*.*

ITEM—I release exonerate and discharge the estate of my deceased brother, Samuel Washington,† from the payment of the money which is due to me for the land I sold to Philip Pendleton (lying in the County of Berkley‡) who assigned the same to him the said Samuel, who by agreement was to pay me therefor.—And whereas by some contract (the purport of which was never communicated to me) between the said Samuel and his son Thornton Washington, the latter became possessed of the aforesaid land without [11] any conveyance having

---

* Robert Alexander, educated in Trinity College, Dublin, opened a high school in the Valley of the Blue Ridge about the year 1749. He called it the "Augusta Academy," and it continued till the Revolution. During that contest its name was changed to Liberty Hall, and in 1782 it was regularly chartered as Liberty Hall Academy. In 1785 it was removed to Rockbridge County, within a short distance of Lexington, and it was there that Washington's legacy was received. In 1798, out of respect to the benefactor, the name was changed to Washington Academy, and in 1803, on the destruction of the old Academy by fire, a new one was located within the limits of Lexington, where it has since remained. The prosperity of the Academy was interrupted by the civil war, and at the peace it was again organized under the presidency of Robert E. Lee, and the name became "The Washington and Lee University."

† Samuel died at Berkley in 1781, aged 47.

‡ In 1772 the county of Frederick was divided into three, forming Frederick, Dunmore and Berkeley counties.

passed

passed from me either to the said Pendleton the said Samuel or the said Thornton and without any consideration having been made, by which neglect neither the legal or equitable title has been alienated;*—it rests therefore with me to declare my intentions concerning the premises—And these are to give and bequeath the said land to whomsoever the said Thornton Washington (who is also dead) devised the same or to his heirs forever, if he died intestate.—Exonerating the estate of the said Thornton, equally with that of the said Samuel from payment of the purchase-money, which with Interest agreeably to the original contract with the said Pendleton would amount to more than a thousand pounds—and whereas two other sons of my said deceased brother Samuel,—namely, George Steptoe Washington and Lawrence Augustine Washington were by the decease of those to whose

---

*"Mr. Pendleton obtained my Deed, or a Bond, or something obligatory upon me, and my heirs, to make him a title to the Land he had of me, & sold to you, upon the purchase money being paid; not one farthing of which has been done— even the last years Rent, if I remember right, which he took upon himself to pay, is yet behind.—However, so soon as I can get evidences I will send a power of attorney to Lund Washton, to make a legal conveyance of the land to you.—In the mean time the Instrument of writing I passed to Mr. Pendleton will always be good against my Heirs, upon the condition of being complied with." *George Washington to Samuel Washington*, 5 October, 1776. Pendleton conveyed to Samuel in 1772. The property was on Bullskin.

care

care they were committed, brought under my protection, and in consequence have occasioned advances on my part for their education at college and other schools for their board *cloathing* and other incidental expenses to the amount of near [12] five thousand dollars over and above the sums furnished by their estate, *wch* sum may be inconvenient for them or their father's Estate to refund —I do for these reasons acquit them and the said Estate from the payment thereof.—My intention being that all accounts between them and me and their father's Estate and me shall stand balanced.—*

ITEM—The balance due to me from the Estate of Bartholomew Dandridge deceased,† (my wife's brother) and which amounted on the first day of October, 1795, to Four hundred and twenty-five pounds (as will appear by an account rendered by his deceased son, John Dandridge, who was the Executor of his father's will) I release and acquit from the payment thereof.—And the *negros* (then thirty three in number) formerly belonging to the

---

* As early as January, 1786, the support of these two boys was at Washington's charge. Many letters from Washington to the boys and their instructors are extant—some being printed in Sparks.

† Sunday, April 24, 1785. "An express arrived with the account of the deaths of Mrs. Dandridge and Mr. B. Dandridge, the mother and brother of Mrs. Washington." *Diary.*

said

said Estate who were taken in Execution,—sold—
and purchased in, on my account in the year
[1795?]* and ever since have remained in the possession and to the use of Mary, widow of the said
Bartholomew Dandridge with their increase, it is
my will and desire shall continue and be in her
possession, without paying hire or making [13]
compensation for the same for the time past or to
come during her natural life, at the expiration of
which, I direct that all of them who are forty years
old and upwards shall receive their freedom, all
under that age and above sixteen shall serve seven
years and no longer, and all under sixteen years
shall serve until they are twenty-five years of age
and then be free.—And to avoid disputes respecting
the ages of any of these *negros* they are to be taken
to the Court of the County in which they reside
and the judgment thereof in this relation shall be
final and a record thereof made, which may be ad-
duced as evidence at any time thereafter if disputes
should arise concerning the same.—And I further
direct that the heirs of the said Bartholomew
Dandridge shall equally share the benefits arising
from the services of the said *negros* according to
the tenor of this devise upon the decease of their
mother.

---

* "Proposals from Mr. Jno. Dandridge, with a list of Slaves in his or his Mother's possession, purchased for and belonging to G. W——n, Sep., 1795," a *MS.* sold at auction 10 December, 1890.

ITEM

ITEM—If Charles Carter who intermarried with my niece, Betty Lewis, is not sufficiently secured in the title to the lots he had of me in the town of Fredericksburg,* it is my will and desire that my Executors shall make such conveyances [14] of them as the law requires to render it perfect.†

ITEM—To my nephew, Wm. Augustine Washington and his heirs (if he should conceive them to be objects worth prosecuting) *and to his heirs* a lot in the town of Manchester (opposite to Richmond) No. 265—drawn on my sole account and also the tenth of one or two hundred acre lots and two or three half acre lots in the city and *vicinity* of Richmond, drawn in partnership with nine others, all in the lottery of the deceased William Byrd are given‡—as is also a lot which

---

* Fredericksburg was erected into a town by an act of Assembly passed in February, 1727. *Hening's Statutes*, iv, 234. It was incorporated in the November session, 1781. Do., x, 439.

† Betty Lewis, daughter of Col. Fielding Lewis and Betty Washington, was born 23 February, 1765; m. Charles Carter, of Culpeper Co., 7 May. 1781; died at Audley in 1829.

‡ "I drew a prize in Col. Byrd's lottery of a half acre lot, No. 265, I believe in the town of Manchester, and I have a lot in some town that was established on James River (below Richmond) by a certain John Wood . . . I am entitled also in partnership with, or the heirs of Peyton Randolph, Richard Randolph, Wm. Fitzhugh of Chatham, George Wythe, Richard Kidder Meade, Lewis Burwell, John Wales, Nathaniel Harrison, Junr , and Thomson Mason, to a tenth part of two or three half acre lots, & 200 acre lots in the aforesaid lottery. But as I purchased

I purchased of John Hood conveyed by William Willie and Samuel Gordon, Trustees of the said John Hood, numbered 139 in the town of Edenburgh in the county of Prince George, State of Virginia.*

ITEM—To my nephew, Bushrod Washington I give and bequeath all the papers in my possession which relate to my civil and military administration of the affairs of this Country:—I leave to him also such of my private papers as are worth preserving;—and at the decease [of my] wife and before, if she is not inclined to retain them, I give and bequeath my library of Books and pamphlets of every kind.†

Thomson Mason (with or without authority) sold this property and never to me at least accounted for an iota of the amount, little I presume is to be expected from this concern." *George Washington to Bushrod Washington*, 29 June, 1796. The managers and trustees of this lottery were John Robinson, Peter Randolph, Peyton Randolph, Presley Thornton, John Page, Charles Carter and Charles Trumbull, and the deed of trust was dated 18 December, 1756. In 1781 all the trustees were dead, Charles Carter alone excepted, and the Legislature passed an act empowering him to give the proper conveyances of lands and tenements. *Hening's Statutes*, x, 446.

* Prince George county was cut out from Charles City county in 1702.

† The papers mentioned in this clause were used by Justice Marshall in the preparation of his *Life of Washington*, and later by Sparks. They were purchased by Congress and deposited in the Department of State.

The library has been scattered, but a number of the volumes were purchased by the Boston Athenæum.

[15]

[15] ITEM—Having sold lands which I possessed in the State of Pennsylvania and part of a tract held in equal right, with George Clinton, late Governor of New York, in the State of New York; —my share of land and interest in the great Dismal Swamp and a tract of land which I owned in the County of Gloucester;—withholding the legal titles thereto until the consideration money should be paid—and having moreover leased and conditionally sold, (as will appear by the tenor of the said leases) all my lands upon the Great *Kanhawa* and the tract upon Difficult Run in the County of Loudon, it is my will and direction that whensoever the contracts are fully and respectively complied with according to the spirit, true intent, and meaning thereof on the part of the purchaser, their heirs, or assigns, that then and in that case conveyances are to be made agreeably to the terms of the said contracts and the money arising therefrom when paid to be vested in Bank stock, the dividends whereof, as of that also which is already vested therein, is to inure to my said wife during her life but the stock it'self is to remain & [16] be subject to the general distribution hereafter directed.

ITEM—To the Earl of Buchan I recommit, "The "Box made of the Oak that sheltered the Great Sir "William Wallace after the battle of Falkirk"*—

---

* The box was presented to the Corporation of Goldsmiths at Edinburgh, which presented it to David Stuart Erskine, the Earl of Buchan, with the freedom of the Company. In a letter presented

presented to me his Lordship in terms too flattering for me to repeat,—with a request "To pass it, on "the event of my decease to the man in my Coun- "try who should appear to merit it best, upon the "same conditions that have induced him to send it "to me"—Whether easy or not to select *the man* who might comport with his Lordship's opinion in this respect, is not for me to say, but conceiving that no disposition of this valuable curiosity, can be more eligible than the re-commitment of it to his own cabinet agreeably to the original design of the Goldsmith's Company of Edinburgh, who presented it to him, and at his request, consented that it should be transferred to me; I do give and bequeath the same to his Lordship, and in case of his decease, to his heir with my grateful thanks for the distinguished honor of presenting it to me, and more especially for the favorable sentiments [17] with which he accomplished it—

---

of 15 September, 1791, the Earl wrote to Washington: "It is a respectable curiosity, and will, I flatter myself, be a relic of long endurance in America, as a mark of that esteem with which I have the honor to be &c." And in the letter which accompanied the box (28 June, 1791) he said: "Feeling my own unworthiness to receive this magnificently significant present, I requested and obtained leave to make it over to the man to whom I thought it most justly due; into your hands I commit it; requesting of you to pass it [as in the will]." In 1791 the bearer of the box, Mr. Archibald Robertson, a portrait painter, reached America, and in January, 1792, the box was placed in the President's hands. Washington's letter of acknowledgment is printed in Sparks, x., 229.

ITEM

ITEM—To my brother Charles Washington I give and bequeath the Gold-headed cane left me by Doct'r Franklin in his will—* I add nothing to it because of the ample provision I have made for his issue—To the acquaintances and friends of my juvenile years, Lawrence Washington and Robert Washington of *Chotanck*,† I give my other two

---

* "My fine crab-tree walking-stick, with a gold head curiously wrought in the form of the cap of liberty, I give to my friend, and the friend of mankind, General Washington. If it were a sceptre, he has merited it, and would become it. It was a present to me from that excellent woman, Madame de Forbach, the Dowager Duchess of Deux-Ponts, connected with some verses which should go with it." *Franklin's Will.* This staff passed to the only surviving son of Charles, Captain Samuel Washington, who transmitted it to his son, Samuel T. Washington. In January, 1843, it was, with a sword of Washington, presented by Samuel T. Washington to Congress. The verses appear to have been lost.

† These were descendants of Lawrence Washington, thus:—

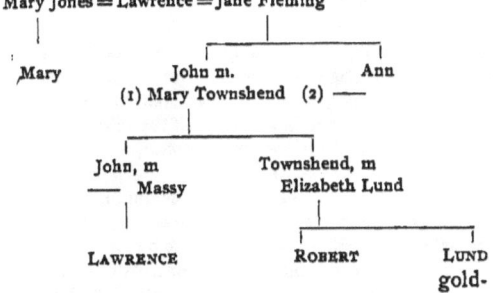

gold-

gold-headed canes, having my arms engraved on them, and to each (as they will be useful where they live), I leave one of the spy glasses which constituted part of my Equipage during the late war*——To my compatriot in arms and old and intimate friend Doct'r Craik, I give my Bureau (or as the Cabinet makers called it Tambour Secretary) and the circular chair, an appendage of my study —To Doct'r David Stuart† I give my large shaving and dressing Table, and my Telescope‡—To the

---

* A spy glass, used by Washington, and made by Jas. Chapman, in London, was sold at auction in Philadelphia, 22 April, 1891. It was inherited by Lawrence Washington, but I doubt if it was the one of those mentioned in the will.

† David Stuart married Nellie [Calvert] Custis, widow of John Parke Custis.

‡ On January 1, 1824, George Washington Parke Custis presented to Andrew Jackson, then President, a pocket telescope, used by Washington during the revolution. "General Jackson received the relic in a manner peculiarly impressive, which showed that however time, hard service and infirmity may have impaired a frame no longer young, the heart was still entire, and alive to the heroic and generous feelings of the soldier, the patriot, and the friend." *National Intelligencer*, quoted in Parton's *Life of Andrew Jackson*, III., 37.

The remarkable number of telescopes in Washington's possession, or so described since his death, led me to suspect that he had an opportunity of looting the stock of some instrument maker, or had access to the laboratory of some institution of learning. The latter was the case. In the Journals of the New York Provincial Congress, under date 8 August, 1776, is the following entry: "A letter from John Berrien and Henry Wilmot,

Reverend

Reverend, now Bryan Lord Fairfax I give a Bible in three large folio volumes with notes, presented to me by the Right Reverend Thomas Wilson, Bishop of Sodor & Man*—To General de la Fayette

Esqrs., dated and received yesterday, was read and filed. They therein mention that they had, by application to the Reverend Mr. Inglis, obtained the telescope belonging to the college for the use of His Excellency General George Washington, and delivered to his aid-de-camp, whom the General had sent to receive it; that Mr. Inglis readily consented to the delivery of it, and the General had been anxious to obtain it."

* This account of the bible was an error on Washington's part. Thomas Wilson, Bishop of Sodor and Man, died 7 March, 1755. In 1785 appeared "The Bible, with notes, by Thomas Wilson, D. D., Lord Bishop of Sodor and Man, and various Renderings, collected from other Translations, by the Rev. Clement Cruttwell, the Editor." *Bath*, 1785, 4to., 3 vols. This was the edition that the son, also named Thomas Wilson, presented to Washington. The presentation must have occurred immediately after the Revolution, for the son died at Bath, in April, 1784. He was chiefly notable by his extravagant appreciation of Mrs. Macaulay, whose statue, in the costume of the goddess of Liberty, he erected in his own church. It is very probable that the bible was sent over at the time that Dr. Wilson sent to Congress a number of copies of his father's works, which were distributed among the delegates. *Journals of Congress*, 22 March, 1785.

These volumes were sold by auction in New York, more than twenty years ago, by order, I am told, of Mr. William H. Corner of Baltimore, who had advanced money upon them. They were purchased by Messrs. Porter and Coates, of Philadelphia, and were in their possession in 1876. Some time after, they were bought for the Library of Congress, and are now there, but inaccessible. Messrs. Porter and Coates write me that each volume contains the signature of Washington, but they cannot

I give

I give a pair of finely wrought steel pistols taken from the enemy in the Revolutionary war—To my sisters in law [18] Hannah Washington,* and

recall any dedication from Dr. Wilson. My thanks are given to Messrs. Porter and Coates, and to Mr. David Hutcheson, of the Library of Congress, for these facts. The library of Mr. Corner was sold at auction in New York, November, 1866, but the Bible is not mentioned in the Catalogue.

After this note was in type I received a letter from Mr. Wilson Miles Cary, of Baltimore, who kindly made inquiries for me in that city, giving the following account:—

"The Rev. Bryan Lord Fairfax left the three volumes by will to the Hon. John C. Herbert (1777-1846), who was the eldest grandson of his sister Sarah, wife of Major John Carlyle. Thus:

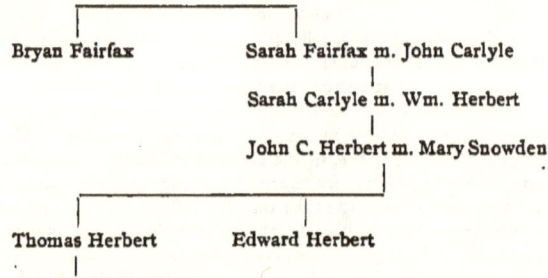

Bryan Fairfax   Sarah Fairfax m. John Carlyle
                          Sarah Carlyle m. Wm. Herbert
                          John C. Herbert m. Mary Snowden

Thomas Herbert   Edward Herbert
  |
Col. Jas. R. Herbert

From John C. Herbert it descended to his son, Edward Herbert, of Baltimore, who, subsequently to the war, being in straitened circumstances, through the medium of Col. Jas. R. Herbert, his nephew, offered the books to Mr. Corner, then a collector of such things."

* Hannah [Bushrod], widow of John Augustine Washington.

Mildred

Mildred Washington;*—To my friends Eleanor Stuart;† Hannah Washington of Fairfield‡ and Elizabeth Washington of Hayfield,‖ I give each a mourning Ring of the value of one hundred dollars—These bequests are not made for the intrinsic value of them, but as *mementos* of my esteem and regard—To Tobias Lear§ I give the use of the farm which he now holds in virtue of a lease from me to him and his deceased wife (for and during their natural lives) free from Rent during his life, at the expiration of which it is to be disposed as is hereafter directed—To Sally B. Haynie (a distant relation of mine) I give and bequeath three hundred dollars¶—To Sarah Green daughter of the deceased Thomas Bishop and to Ann Walker, daughter of John Alton,** also deceased I give each one hundred dollars, in consideration of the attachment of their father[s] to me, each of whom having lived

---

* Mildred [Thornton], widow of Charles Washington.

† Eleanor Calvert, widow of John Parke Custis, and wife of Doctor David Stuart.

‡ Hannah [Fairfax], wife of Warren Washington.

‖ Elizabeth [Foote], widow of Lund Washington.

§ Lear came to Mount Vernon 29 May, 1786, as private secretary to the General, and tutor to Washington Custis. In 1795 a perpetual lease of 360 acres was made to Tobias and Frances Lear.

¶ Sally Ball Haynie was the daughter of Elizabeth Haynie.

** Alton and Bishop were old servants of Washington.

nearly

nearly forty years in my family.—To each of my nephews William Augustine Washington, George Lewis, George Steptoe Washington, Bushrod Washington, and Samuel Washington, I give one of the swords or *cutteaux* of which I may die pos[19] sessed, and they are to *chuse* in the order they are named.—These swords are accompanied with an injunction not to unsheath them for the purpose of shedding blood except it be for self defence, or in defence of their Country and it's rights, and in the latter case to keep them unsheathed, and prefer falling with them in their hands to the relinquishment thereof.*

---

* The history of these swords is by no means easy to write. In 1843 Col. George Corbin Washington, of Georgetown, wrote to George W. Summers, a member of Congress, that he had in his possession two of the swords, the one devised to him by his father, William Augustine Washington, and the other by his uncle, Judge Bushrod Washington. There were others in the possession of George Lewis and George Steptoe Washington, and the fifth was offered by Samuel T. Washington, a son of Samuel, to the government (1843). "My father," continued George C. Washington, "was entitled to the first choice under the will, but was prevented by indisposition from attending at Mount Vernon when the distribution took place, and Judge Washington selected for him the most finished and costly sword, with which associations were connected highly complimentary to General Washington; but I often heard my father say that he would have preferred the sword selected by Colonel Samuel Washington, from the fact that it was used by the General during the revolutionary war. I have at different times heard similar statements as to this fact made by Colonel

Having

AND NOW,

Having gone through these specific devises, with explanations for the more correct understanding of the meaning and design of them, I proceed to the distribution of the more important parts of my Estate, in manner following

Samuel Washington, Judge Washington, and Major Lawrence Lewis, and am not aware that it has been questioned by any member of the family. The sword was represented to me as being a couteau, with a plain green ivory handle." This particular sword was said to have been worn by Washington during the Revolution, and again 1794, when he took command of the army against the Whiskey Insurrection. This sword is now in the Department of State, Washington. "The handle is of ivory, colored a pale green, and wound spirally at wide intervals with silver wire. It was manufactured by J. Bailey, Fishkill, Dutchess County, New York, and has the maker's name engraved upon the hilt." Custis, *Recollections*, 160.

A second sword was at Mount Vernon in 1859, and was described by Lossing, as "the Spanish dress-sword worn by Washington when he was President of the United States, and which appears in Stuart's full length portrait of him at that time. It has a finely gilt hilt, and black leather scabbard, gilt mounted. On one side of the blade are the words RECTI FAC ET ICE (?)— 'Do what is right;' on the other, NEMINEM TIMEAS—'Fear no man.'" This sword, in a much injured condition, was sold at auction in Philadelphia, 22 April, 1891, for $1100. The catalogue states: "During the late civil war, this sword, with a lot of other valuables, was hid in a pigeon house, where it was so injured by rust that the scabbard was destroyed and the blade so rusted that it obliterated the inscription. About five inches of the lower portion of the blade has been broken off, but is joined to the other part of the blade by a gold band. The

First—

First—To my nephew Bushrod Washington and his heirs (partly in consideration of an intimation to his deceased father, while we were bachelors and he had kindly undertaken to superintend my Estate, during my military services in the former war between Great Britain and France, that if I should fall therein, Mt. Vernon (then less extensive in dominion than at present, should become his

---

gold-plated top of the scabbard is missing. The hilt of the sword, and other trappings, are gold plated." This sword was the one selected by Judge Bushrod Washington.

A third sword, that selected by George Steptoe Washington. is now in the possession of Miss Alice L. Riggs, of Washington, D. C. It was made by Theophilus Alt, of Solingen, Germany, and sent to America in charge of his son, who was to present it to Washington. The young man upon reaching America, fell into bad hands, was frightened out of his purpose, and pawning the sword, went into the interior. Washington had noticed an announcement in the gazettes that a sword of masterly workmanship was about to be presented to him by a celebrated foreign artist, as an evidence of his veneration, &c. "I thought no more of the matter afterwards, until a gentleman with whom I have no acquaintance, coming from and going to I know not where, at a tavern I never could get information of, came across this sword (for it is presumed to be the same), pawned for thirty dollars, which he paid, left it in Alexandria, nine miles from my house in Virginia, with a person who refunded him the money, and sent the sword to me. This is all I have been able to learn of this curious affair. The blade is highly wrought, and decorated with many military emblems. It has my name engraved thereon, and the following inscription, translated from the Dutch, '*Condemner of despotism, Preserver of Liberty, glorious Man, take from my Son's hands this Sword, I beg

property)

property) I give and bequeath all that part thereof which is comprehen[20]ded within the following limits—viz:—Beginning at the ford of Dogue Run near my mill and extending along the road and bounded thereby as it now goes, and ever has gone since my recollection of it, to the ford of little hunting Creek, at the gum spring until it comes to a knowl opposite to an old road which formerly

---

you. A. SOLLINGEN.' The hilt is either gold, or richly plated with that metal, and the whole carries with it the form of a horseman's sword or long sabre." *Washington to John Quincy Adams*, 12 September, 1796. This sword also has suffered much "owing to burial during the late war, by the Washingtons." It was among the relics exhibited at New York, in 1889.

A fourth sword, that selected for William Augustine Washington, passed into the possession of his son George Corbin Washington, and from him to that of Lewis William Washington. His wife, Ella Bassett Washington, sold it, with other relics, to the State Library of New York, where it now is. It is described in the Report of the Library for 1873, as the "dress sword of Washington." It is a "straight pointed blade, with hilt and chain of polished steel, dotted with steel beads. The present case of green Turkey morocco is not the original; that was of white shagreen or shark skin. It was cleaned and covered in 1854 in Baltimore by S. Jackson, cutler."

To the New York Exhibition of 1889, Miss Virginia T. Lewis, of Baltimore, contributed a dress sword, described as follows: "It has a handsome filagree handle and guard, with sword-knot to correspond; the rapier-blade sheathed in a sheepskin or white parchment scabbard, which is silver-mounted. Washington wore this sword when resigning his commission as Commander-in-chief of the army in Annapolis, December 23, 1783, and when inaugurated in New York, April 30, 1789, and afterward on all
passed

passed through the lower field of Muddy-Hole Farm; at which, on the north side of the said road are three red or Spanish oaks marked as a corner, and a stone placed—thence by a line of trees to be marked rectangular. to the black line, or outer boundary of the tract between Thomson Mason and myself,—thence with that line easterly, (*now double* ditching with a post and rail fence thereon)

---

state and dress occasions." This is probably the sword received by George Lewis, though I am unable to identify it positively, no reply being received to my inquiries.

A sword was exhibited in New York, in 1889, as one that had been presented to Washington by Major-General William Darke. Upon application to Mr. Thornton A. Washington, who exhibited the sword, he very courteously gave me the following information: "The sword was not one of the five swords mentioned in George Washington's will. It, together with a suit of clothes, was presented by G. W. in person, to Lawrence Augustine Washington, a nephew of his, and a son of his oldest full brother Col. Samuel Washington, late of Harewood, Berkeley Co., now Jefferson Co., West Virginia. This Lawrence A. Washington, together with a brother, George Steptoe Washington, were left orphans by the death of their father, the said Col. Samuel, in the fall of 1781 . . . On the death of Lawrence A. Washington, about 1824, the sword and suit went to his son of the same name. He, the last named L. A. W., after graduating at the medical college in Philadelphia, removed with his family to Texas, and died there about ten years ago, and his widow, Mrs. Martha D. Washington, who had become impoverished by the war, and who became the owner of these relics, placed them in my hands for sale. They had never been on any public exhibition. They are now the property of the Washington Association, at Morristown, New Jersey."

to

to the run of little hunting Creek, thence with that run, which is the boundary of the lands of the late Humphrey Peake and *me*, to the tide water of the said Creek thence by that water to Potomac River, thence with the River to the mouth of Dogue Creek, and thence with the said Dogue Creek to the place of beginning, at the aforesaid ford, containing upwards of Four thousand acres, be the same more or less together with the Mansion House, [21] and all other buildings and *improvemt[s]* thereon.—

Secondly—In consideration of the consanguinity between them and my wife, being as nearly related to her as to myself, as on account of the affection I had for, and the obligation I was under to their father when living, who from his youth had attached himself to my person and followed my fortunes through the vicissitudes of the late Revolution, afterwards devoting his time to the superintendence of my private concerns for many years whilst my public employments rendered it impracticable for me to do it myself, thereby affording me essential services, and always performing them in a manner the most filial and respectful; for these reasons I say, I give and bequeath to George Fayette Washington and Lawrence Augustine Washington* & their heirs my Estate East of little

---

*Sons of Major George Augustine Washington and Frances Bassett. George Fayette was the second of that name. It is

hunting creek lying on the River Potomac, including the farm of 360 acres, leased to Tobias Lear as noticed before and containing in the whole, by deeds, Two thousand & twenty seven acres be it more or less which said Estate, it is my will and desire should be equitably and advantageously divided between them, according to quantity, quality & other circumstances when [22] the youngest shall have arrived at the age of twenty one years, by three judicious and disinterested men, one to be chosen by each of the brothers and the third by these two,—In the mean time if the termination of my wife's interest therein should have ceased the profits, arising therefrom are to be applied for their joint uses and benefit.

Third—And whereas it has always been my intention, since my expectation of having issue has ceased, to consider the grand children of my wife in the same light as I do my own relations and to act a friendly part by them, more especially by the two whom we have reared from their earliest infancy, namely, Eleanor Parke Custis and George Washington Parke Custis; and whereas the former of these hath lately intermarried with Lawrence Lewis, a son of my deceased sister Betty Lewis, by

---

not a little remarkable that Washington should have written Lawrence Augustine Washington for Charles Augustine Washington. Lawrence Augustine Washington was the son of Samuel Washington.

which

which union the inducement to provide for them both has been increased.—Wherefore I give and bequeath to the said Lawrence Lewis and Eleanor Parke Lewis, his wife, and their heirs, the residue of my Mount Vernon Estate, not already devised to my nephew Bushrod Washington comprehended within the fol[23]lowing description.—viz—all the land north of the Road leading from the ford of Dogue Run to the Gum Spring as described in the devise of the other part of the tract to Bushrod Washington until it comes to the stone and three red or Spanish oaks on the knowl.—thence with the rectangular line to the back line (between Mr. Mason and *me*)—thence with that line westerly, along the new double ditch to Dogue Run, by the tumbling dam of my mill,—thence with the said Run to the ford aforementioned;—to which I add all the land I possess west of the said Dogue Run & Dogue Crk bonded, Easterly & Southerly thereby—together with the mill, Distillery and all other houses and improvements on the premises making together about two thousand acres be it more or less.

Fourth—Actuated by the principle already mentioned, I give and bequeath to George Washington Parke Custis the Grand son of my wife and my ward and to his heirs, the tract I hold on four mile Run in the *vicinity* of Alexandria containing one
thousd

thousd two hundred acres more or less*;—and my entire square, numbering twenty one, in the city of Washington.

[24] *Fifth*—All the rest and residue of my Estate, real and personal, not disposed of in manner aforesaid—In whatsoever consisting—wheresoever lying, and wheresoever found—a Schedule of which as far as is recollected, with a reasonable estimate of its value is hereunto annexed—I desire may be sold by my Executors at such times—in such manner, and in such credits (if an equal valid and satisfactory distribution of the specific property cannot be made without) as, in their judgment shall be most conducive to the interests of the parties concerned; and the monies arising therefrom to be divided into twenty three equal parts and applied as follows—viz:—

To William Augustine Washington, Elizabeth Spotswood, Jane Thornton, and the heirs of Ann Ashton;† son and daughters of my deceased brother

---

*A fac-simile of a survey by Washington of this tract is printed in Custis, *Recollections and Private Memoirs of Washington*, 445.

†William Augustine, born at Wakefield, 25 November, 1757, married (1) his cousin Jane, daughter of John Augustine Washington, 25 September, 1777; (2) Mary, daughter of Richard Henry Lee, 10 July, 1792; (3) —— Taylor, 11 May, 1799; died at Georgetown, Va.; October, 1810. Elizabeth, born at Wakefield, about 1750; married Alexander Spotswood. Jane, born at Wakefield, about 1752, married Col. —— Thornton. Ann, born

Augustine

Augustine Washington, I give and bequeath four parts—that is—one part to each of them.

To Fielding Lewis, George Lewis, Robert Lewis, Howell Lewis, & Betty Carter, sons and daughter of my deceased sister Betty Lewis I give & bequeath five other parts—one to each of them.

To George Steptoe Washington, Lawrence Augustine Washington, Harriot [25] Parks,* and the heirs of Thornton Washington,† sons and daughter of my deceased brother Samuel Washington, I give and bequeath other four parts, one part to each of them.—‡

---

at Wakefield, about 1755; married Burdet Ashton, of Westmoreland county; and had one child who lived—Sarah Ashton.

*Married 4 July, 1796, Andrew Parks, of Baltimore.

† He left three sons.

‡ Another son of Samuel had incurred Washington's displeasure because of his extravagance, and was the subject of the following letter:—

TO MR. ROBERT CHAMBERS.

MOUNT VERNON, 28 Jan. 1789.

Sir,

I have received your letter of the 12th Inst: enclosing your account against Mr Ferdinand Washington which is herewith returned—and must inform you that I have repeatedly refused, and am determined not to have any thing to do in the settlement of his affairs, for his conduct, while living, was such as I totally disapproved of, and left no means or advice unessayed to counteract—His extravagance could not be unknown to those who had dealings with him, and particularly for any length of

To

To Corbin Washington, and the heirs of Jane Washington,* I give and bequeath two parts;—one part to each of them;—

To Samuel Washington, Frances Ball,† & Mildred Hammond,‡ son and daughters of my brother Charles Washington I give and bequeath three parts—one part to each of them.—And to George Fayette Washington, Charles Augustine Washington and Maria Washington, sons and daughter of my deceased nephew, Geo: Augustine Washington, I give one other part—that is—to each a third of that part.

To Elizabeth Parke Law,∥ Martha Parke Peter,§

---

time;—they therefore who gave credit, and especially for such Articles as were not necessary for his Support, must have been sensible, at the time, of the risque which they took upon themselves, and consequently can have no person to reproach with having drawn them into it.—The Administrators must settle his affairs in the manner which appears most proper to them without my interference in any respect.

I am &c.   G. WASHINGTON.

* See *ante*, p. 114.

† Married Col. Burges Ball.

‡ Mildred, daughter of Charles Washington, born 1777, married Col. Thomas Hammond. *Hayden.*

∥ A sister of Nellie Custis, born 21 August, 1776, and married 16 January, 1795, Mr. Law, a nephew of Lord Ellenborough.

§ Born 31 December, 1777, and married Thomas Peter.

and

and Eleanor Parke Lewis,* I give and bequeath three other parts—that is, a part to each of them.†

And to my nephew Bushrod Washington & Lawrence Lewis,—and to my ward, the grandson of my wife,‡ I give and bequeath one other part; —that is a third part to each of them—And if it should so happen, that any of the persons whose names are here enumerated (unknown to me) should now [26] be deceased, or should die before me, that in either of these cases, the heirs of such deceased person shall, notwithstanding derive all the benefit of the bequest, in the same manner as if he, or she was actually living at the time.

And by way of advice, I recommend it to my Executors not to be precipitate in disposing of the landed property (herein directed to be sold) if from temporary causes the sale thereof should be dull,

---

*Born 21 March, 1779, and married Lawrence Lewis, the nephew of General Washington.

† The three ladies mentioned in this clause were daughters of John Parke Custis (son of Mrs. Washington, by her first husband) and Nellie Calvert. Receiving no response to some inquiries made in courteous terms with stamp for reply of Mr. Edmund Law Rogers, of Baltimore, I turned for information to the Rev. Horace Edwin Hayden, of Wilkesbarre, Pa., and was not disappointed. His work in Virginia genealogies constitutes one of the most valuable records that time and patience could collect. I have expressed my particular obligations to his courtesy in other places; but make this general one as an index of the extent of those obligations.

‡ George Washington Parke Custis.

land

experience having fully evinced, that the price of land (especially above the Falls of the Rivers & on the Western Waters) have been progressively rising, and cannot be long checked in its increasing value.—and I particularly recommend it to such of the Legatees (under this clause of my will) as can make it convenient, to take each a share of my stock in the Potomac Company in preference to the amount of what it might sell for; being thoroughly convinced myself, that no uses to which the money can be applied will be so productive as the Tolls arising from this navigation when in full operation (and this from the nature of things it must be 'ere long) and more especially if that of the Shenandoah is added thereto.

[27] The family Vault at Mount Vernon requiring repairs, and being improperly situated besides, I desire that a new one of Brick, and upon a larger scale, may be built at the foot of what is commonly called the Vineyard Inclosure,—on the ground which is marked out.—In which my remains, with those of my deceased relatives (now in the Old Vault) and such others of my family as may *chuse* to be entombed there, may be deposited. —And it is my express desire that my corpse may be interred in a private manner, without parade or funeral oration.*

---

*Washington died on the night of Saturday, 14 December, 1799. On Sunday a mahogany coffin was obtained of Henry &

Lastly—

Lastly—I constitute and appoint my dearly beloved wife Martha Washington, my nephews William Augustine Washington, Bushrod Washington, George Steptoe Washington, Samuel Washington & Lawrence Lewis, & my ward, George Washington Parke Custis, (when he shall have arrived at the age of twenty years) Executrix and Executors of this Will & Testament,—In the construction of

Joseph Ingle, of Alexandria, "with silver plate, engraved, furnished with lace, handles and a covered case with lifters." So the undertakers described the coffin. Custis says it was lined with lead, and "upon it was placed at the head, an ornament inscribed SURGE AD JUDICIUM; about the middle of the coffin, GLORIA DEO; and on a small silver plate, in the form of the American shield, were the words:

GEORGE WASHINGTON,
Born Feb. 22, 1732
Died December 14, 1799."

The funeral occurred on Wednesday, the eighteenth, and the order of procession is given in Custis's *Recollections*, 478 *note*. The body was deposited in the old burial vault, where it remained till the new one was constructed in accordance with the terms of the will, many years after (1830–1). In 1837, Mr. John Struthers, of Philadelphia, presented marble coffins, each cut from a solid block of Pennsylvania marble, and at his suggestion an antechamber to the new vault was constructed in which these marble coffins rest. An interesting record of the transfer of the remains to their final resting-place was left by Mr. Strickland, who was present. It is printed in part in Winneberger's *Home of Washington*, and Lossing's work of the same title. The *Churchman* (date?) printed a letter from Jane C. Washington on this incident, as well as on the first transfer in 1830, from the old vault to the new.

which

which it will readily be perceived that no professional character has been consulted or has had any agency in the draught—and that, although it has occupied [28] many of my leisure hours to digest & to *through* it into its present form, it may notwithstanding, appear crude and incorrect—But having endeavored to be plain and explicit in all the Devises—even at the expense of prolixity, perhaps of tautology, I hope, and trust, that no disputes will arise concerning them; but if contrary to expectation the case should be otherwise from the want of legal expression, or the usual technical terms, or because too much or too little, has been said on any of the devises to be consonant with law, my will and direction expressly is, that all disputes (if unhappily any should arise) shall be decided by three impartial and intelligent men, known for their probity and good understanding; two to be chosen by the disputants, each having the choice of one, and the third by those two.—which three men thus chosen, shall unfettered by Law, or legal constructions declare their sense of the Testator's intention; and such decision is, to all intents and purposes to be as binding on the Parties as if it had been given in the Supreme Court of the United States.

[29] In witness of all and of each of the things herein contained I have set my hand and seal this ninth day of July, in the year one thousand seven hundred

hundred and ninety [nine*] and of the Independence of the United States, the Twenty fourth.

G? WASHINGTON.

SCHEDULE OF PROPERTY† *comprehended in the foregoing Will, which is directed to be sold, and some of it, conditionally is sold; with descriptive and explanitory notes relative thereto.—*

IN VIRGINIA

	Acres	Price	Dollars
LOUDOUN COUNTY—			
Difficult Run	300		6.666 (a)

(a) This tract for the size of it is valuable; more for it's situation than the quality of it's soil, though that is good for farming, with a considerable portion of gr'd that might, very easily, be improved into meadow.—It *lyes* on the great Road from the City of Washington, Alexandria and George Town to *Leesburgh* & Winchester, at Difficult bridge—nine-

---

*A word omitted by Washington. It is noteworthy that the will was not signed in the presence of witnesses.

† I have thrown the schedule and notes together, for the convenience of reference.

teen

teen miles from Alexandria—less from the City & George Town, and not more than three from Matildaville at the Great Falls of Potomac—

There is a valuable seat on the premises—and the whole is conditionally sold for the sum annexed in the schedule.

LOUDOUN & FAUQUIER

Ashby's Bent	2.481	10	24.810	(b)
Chattin's Run	885	8	7.080	

(b) What the selling prices of lands in the *vicinity* of these two tracts are I know not; but compared with those above the ridge, and others below them the value annexed will appear moderate—a less one would not obtain them from me.—

BERKLEY—

So. Fork of Bullskin	1600
Head of Evan's M	453
In Wormley's Line	183
	2236 20 44.720 (c)

(c) The surrounding land, not superior in soil, situation or properties of any sort, sell currently at from twenty to thirty dollars an acre.—The lowest price is affixed to these.

FREDERICK—

FREDERICK—
  Bought from Mercer*   571   20   11.420 (*d*)
  (*d*) The observations made in the last note applies equally to this tract being in the *vicinity* of them, and of similar quality, *altho* it lye's in another County.

HAMPSHIRE—
  (*e*) On Potk River above B. 240   15   3.600 (*e*)
  This tract though small, is extremely valuable—it *lyes* on the Potomac River, about twelve miles above the Town of Bath (or Warm Springs) and it is in the shape of a horse-shoe, the River running almost around it.—Two hundred acres of it *is* rich low grounds ; with a great abundance of the largest and finest Walnut Trees, which with the produce of the soil might (by means of the improved navigation of the Potomac) be brought to a shipping port with more ease and at *a* smaller expense than that which is transported 30 miles, only by land.

GLOUCESTER—
  On North River   400 *abt*   3.600 (*f*)
  (*f*) This tract is of second rate Gloucester

---

*James Francis Mercer, to whom Washington wrote some very spicy letters upon his shortcomings. The land was taken for a debt owing to Washington.

low

low ground—it has no improvement thereon, but *lyes* on navigable water abounding in fish and oysters : it was received in payment of a debt (carrying interest) and valued in the year 1789, by an impartial gentleman *to* £800—N. B. it has *lettely* been sold and there is due thereon, a balance equal to what is annexed—the Schedule.*

---

*WASHINGTON TO COLO. WARNER LEWIS.

MOUNT VERNON, 19 December, 1788.

Dear Sir,

As it has happened that the only mode by which a pretty considerable debt wh^h is due to me, can be discharged with any convenience to the Estate that owes it, is to receive a small tract of Land in Gloucester County and I believe not far from you in payment; May I take the liberty of requesting the favor of you to give me your opinion of its worth with a short detail of the quality of the soil growth thereon—proportion and sort of Woodland to that which is cleared—Improvements (if any)—with the advantages and disadvantages attending its local Situation.

The following description of it I have had from the Gentleman who wishes me to take it—see Mr John Dandridges letter dated 6th December 88.

Of two evils which present themselves to my view in the present case namely to distress a worthy family, or take Land wh^h I do not want in lieu of Money which I really do want I prefer the latter—The gentleman thinks worth £1000. For a farthing less than it is worth, I do not desire to possess it; but I wish this to be ascertained by a disinterested gentleman in whose judgment I can confide—for this reason I appeal to you

NANSEMOND—

NANSEMOND—
  Near Suffolk ⅓ of
    1119 acres   373   8   2.984 (*g*)
  (*g*) These 373 acres *are* the third part of undivided purchases made by the deceased Fielding Lewis, Thomas Walker and myself, on full conviction that they would become valuable.—the land *lye's* on the road from Suffolk to Norfolk touches (if I am not mistaken) some part of the navigable water of Nansemond River—borders on—and comprehends part of the rich Dismal Swamp; is capable of great improvement;—and from it's situation must become extremely valuable.
GREAT DISMAL SWAMP.
  My dividend thereof   abt 20.000 (*h*)
  (*h*) This is an undivided interest *wch* I

without offering an apology for the trouble it must necessarily give you to comply with my request.

Butler says "every thing is worth what it will fetch" but in these times of Scarcity every thing will not fetch what it is worth—and it is for that reason I have asked your opinion respecting the latter.—to which I pray you to add to what amount you conceive it would be rented, for as to selling, I presume it is entirely out of the question I mean for cash at the sum fixed for or it would not have been offered to me, it being well known to the present proprietor that to take the land is solely to accomodate the Estate for which he acts.

                I am &c.   G. WASHINGTON.
                                            held

held in the Great Dismal Swamp Company, containing about 400 acres, with my part of the Plantation and Stock thereon belonging to the Company [in the s'd Swamp.*

OHIO RIVER

Round Bottom †	587	10
Little Kanhawa	2,314	
16 miles lower down	2,448	
Opposite Big Bent	4,395	
	9,744	10 97,440 (*i*)

(*i*) These several tracts of land are of the

---

* Washington owned two of twenty-one shares in the Great Dismal Swamp Company, which he valued in 1793 at £5000. The Company in 1762 took up 40,000 acres in the interior and richest part of the swamp.

† "Having mentioned the name of Cresap, it reminds me of another matter which I must also request the favor of you to give me information upon. It is, whether, if he has had any surveys returned to the Land Office of this State, there is one for about five or six hundred acres for a tract which is well known and distinguished by the name of the Round Bottom on the Ohio, opposite to Pipe Creek, and a little above a creek called Capteening? He has, I find, arrested my survey of it for 587 acres, made under all the legal forms, and upon proper warrants, for no better reason that I could ever learn, than because it has a good bottom and convenient for him to possess it, and had it in his power to do it with impunity." *Washington to John Harvie*, 10 February, 1784. See my *Washington*, II., 295, 392, 410.

first

first quality on the Ohio River in the parts where they are situated; being almost, if not altogether, River bottoms.

The smallest of these Tracts is actually sold at ten dollars an acre, but the consideration therefor not received, the rest are equally valuable, and will sell as high, especially that which *lye's* just below the little Kanhawa, and is opposite to a thick settlement on the west side the River.

The four tracts have an aggregate breadth upon the River of Sixteen miles and is bounded thereby that distance.*

---

* To encourage enlistments for the Virginia regiment designed to repel the trespasses of the French on the Ohio, Governor Dinwiddie issued a proclamation dated 19 February, 1754, offering 200,000 acres of land, to be divided among the officers and soldiers. By an order of Council, 15 December, 1769, surveys were made, and patents issued by Lord Dunmore. Washington was much interested in the matter, and, indeed, was the prime mover in inducing the Colony to fulfill its promise. In August, 1770, at Captain Weedon's, he met the officers of the old Virginia regiment; and in the following October, he made a journey to the Ohio to locate the grants in the interest of those who held patents. The journal of this tour is printed in my *Washington*, II., 285-316. Delays and difficulties occurred in completing the grant, owing in part to the conflicting claims of the Walpole grant, and it was not until November, 1772, that the certificates of surveys were lodged in the Secretary's office. A part of the claims were then satisfied, and Washington obtained
GREAT

GREAT KANHAWA—
Near the mouth west	10,990	
East Side above	7,276	
Mouth of Cole River	2,000	
Opposite thereto	2,950	
Burning Spring	125	
	23,341	200,000 (*k*)

(*k*) These tracts are situated on the Great *Kanhawa* River, and the first four are

patents for "upwards of twenty thousand acres of land on the Ohio and Great Kanhawa (ten thousand of which are situated on the banks of the first mentioned river, between the mouths of the two Kanhawas, and the remainder on the Great Kanhawa, or New River, from the mouth, or near it, upwards, in one continued survey)." *Advertisement*, 15 July, 1773. These appear to have been obtained in his own right, but fell short of his allowance by five thousand acres, and did not include another five thousand acres, the rights to which he had purchased from Captain Posey and Lieutenant Thruston.

Under the proclamation of 19 February, 1754, Washington obtained warrants for

10,990 acres in Fincastle county.

4,395 ⎫
2,448 ⎬ in Botetourt county.
2,314 ⎭

These lands were surveyed, and patents granted by Lord Dunmore, 15 December, 1772, the patents exempting the land from any quit rents for fifteen years from the date of issue. "In the month of March, 1774, I encountered *in preparation only*, an expence of at least £300; by the purchase of Servants, nails, tools and other necessaries for the purpose of seating and cultivating the above lands, agreeably to our Act of Assembly; bound

bound thereby for more than forty miles.
—It is acknowledged by all who have seen them (and of the tract containing 10,990 acres which I have been on myself, I can assert*) that there is no richer, or more valuable land in all that Region;
—They are conditionally sold for the sum mentioned in the schedule—that is, 200,000 dollars and if the terms of that sale are not complied with, they will

---

and for transporting the same over the Allighaney Mountains—but this was entirely sunk. The disturbances occasioned by the Indians, which immediately followed, put a stop to my proceedings—the servants, some of them, engaged in the Militia—others squandered—and the whole were lost *to me;* while my Goods, as I am informed, were seized for the use of the Militia, and a fort which was built, upon the Expedition under Lord Dunmore, and no compensation made me for them—nor, if I am rightly informed, anything given upon which I can found a claim.

"The March following I went through the second edition of a similar expence, and find by having recourse to my papers (since I came home) the certificates which I enclose herewith." *Washington to Edmund Randolph*, 18 March, 1784. The details of these expeditions will be found in my collection of *Washington's Writings*, II., 451, 459; III., 128.

* The original grant of this tract, dated 6 July, 1784, and signed by Gov. Benjamin Harrison, together with three surveys and plans of the land, were sold at auction in Philadelphia, April, 1891.

See letter of Washington to David Stuart, inserted after this will.

command

command considerable more.—The tract of which the 125 acres is a moiety, was taken up by General Andrew Lewis and myself for on account of a bituminous spring, which it contains, of so inflammable a nature as to burn as freely as spirits, and is as nearly difficult to extinguish.

MARYLAND—

Charles County	600	6	3.600 (*l*)
Montgomery County	519	12	6.228 (*m*)

(*l*) I am but little acquainted with this land, although I have once been on it.—It was receiv'd (many years since) in discharge of a debt due to me from Daniel Jenifer Adams, at the value annexed thereto, and must be worth more.—It is very level, *lyes* near the River Potomac.

(*m*) This tract *lyes* about 30 miles above the City of Washington not far from *Kittoctan*.—It is good farming land, and by those who are well acquainted with it I am informed that it would sell at twelve or $15 p^r acre.*

---

* Known as Woodstock Manor. It was conveyed to Washington 1 April, 1793, by John Francis Mercer and Sophia, his wife, and James Stewart and Rebecca, his wife.

PENNSYLVANIA—

PENNSYLVANIA—
    Great Meadows   234   6   1.404 (*n*)
    (*n*) This land is valuable on account of it's local situation and other properties.—It affords an exceeding good stand on Braddock's Road from Fort Cumberland to *Pittsburgh* and besides a fertile soil possesses a large quantity of natural meadow fit for the scythe.—It is distinguished by the appellation of the Great Meadows, where the first action with the French in the year 1754 was fought.*

NEW YORK—
    Mohawk River *abt*   1000   6   6.000 (*o*)
    (*o*) This is the moiety of about 2000 *acres* which remains unsold of 6071 acres on the Mohawk River, (Montgomery Ct'y) in a Patent granted to Daniel Coxe in the Township of *Coxebourgh & Carolaca* as will appear by deed from Marinus Willet & wife to George Clinton (late Governor of New York) and myself ; the latter sales have been at six dollars an acre and what remains unsold will *fetch* that, or more.†

---

* Crawford, on 6 December, 1770, announced to Washington that he had purchased the Great Meadows from Mr. Harrison for thirty pistoles.

† "I am sorry we have been disappointed in our expectation
                                                          NORTH

NORTH WEST TERRITORY—

On little Miami	839
Ditto	977
Ditto	1235

3051   5   15.251 (*p*)

(*p*) The quality of these lands & their situation may be known by the surveyor's certificates, which are filed along with the patents—They *lye* in the *vicinity* of Cincinnati, one tract near the mouth of the little Miami, another seven, & the third ten miles up the same—I have been informed that they will readily command more than they are estimated at.—

KENTUCKY—

Rough Creek	3,000
Ditto adjoin'g	2,000

5,000   2   10.000 (*q*)

(*q*) For the description of these tracts in detail, see General Spottswood's letters

---

of the mineral spring at Saratoga; and of the purchase of that part of the Oriskany tract, on which Fort Schuyler stands; but very glad you have succeeded upon such advantageous terms in the purchase of six thousand acres adjoining; for you certainly have obtained it amazingly cheap." *Washington to Governor Clinton*, 25 November, 1784.

filed

filed with the other papers relating to them—Besides the general good quality of the land, there is a valuable bank of Iron Ore thereon;—which when the settlement becomes more populous (and settlers are moving that way very fast) will be found very valuable, as the rough creek, a branch of Green River affords ample water for furnaces and forges.

LOTS.

CITY OF WASHINGTON—

Two near the *Capital Sqr* 634 Cost $963, and with *Buildgs*.	15.000 (*r*)
No. 5, 12, 13, & 14, the 3 last water lots on the Eastern Branch in Sqr. 667, containing together 34, 438 Sqr. feet at 12 cts.	4.132 (*s*)

(*r*) The two lots near the *Capital* in Square 634, cost me $963 only, but in this price I was favored on condition that I should build two brick houses, three storys high each;—without this reduction, the selling price of those lots would have cost me about $1350.

—These lots with the buildings thereon when completed will stand me in $15,-000 at least.

(*s*)

(*s*) Lots No. 5, 12, 13 & 14 on the Eastern Branch are advantageously situated on the water, and although many lots much less convenient, have sold a great deal higher, I will rate these at 12 cts the square foot only.*

ALEXANDRIA—

Corner of Pitt and Prince Strts half an acre—laid out into buildgs 3 or 4 of *wch* are let on *grd* Rent at $3 pr foot } 4.000 (*t*)

(*t*) For this lot, though unimproved I have refused $3500, it has since been

---

*I applied to Col. O. H. Ernst, at present in charge of the public buildings and grounds in Washington, for the exact locality of these lots. He has kindly sent me the following:

"The records of this office show that Washington acquired title to the whole of Square 21; to Lot No. 16—not two lots, as you have it—in Square 634; to Lots 5, 12, 13 and 14 in Square 667; and to Lots 4, 5 and 6 in square east of Square 667.

"The boundaries of Square 21 are D and E Sts. North, and 25th and 26th Sts. West.

"The boundaries of Square 634 are B and C Sts. North, Capitol St. and New Jersey Ave.

"The boundaries of Square 667 are U and V Sts. South, First St. West and Water St.

"The boundaries of square east of Square 667 are U and V Sts. South, Water St. and the Eastern Branch. This square was under water at the time. Lots 4, 5 and 6 were opposite Lots 12, 13 and 14 in the adjoining Square—667—and were of value only as securing beyond peradventure the water front appertaining to the lots in Square 667."

laid

laid off into proper sized lots for building on, three or four of which are let on ground Rent forever at three dollars a foot on the street, and this price is asked for both fronts on Pitt and Princess Streets.*

WINCHESTER—

A lot in the Town, of half an acre & another on the Commons of about 6 acres—supposed } 400 (*u*)

(*u*) As neither the lot in the Town or common have any improvements on them it is not easy to fix a price, but as both are well situated it is presumed the price annexed to them in the Schedule is a reasonable *valu*.

---

*On this section Mr. Cassius F. Lee, of Alexandria, writes me:—

"The half square of ground in this city owned by Washington was on the corner of *Prince* and Pitt streets. It is covered with dwellings, and is in the best part of the town, and a square only east of the post office, which is on Prince street. Prince street is the correct name. Washington also owned a quarter square on Cameron street, and on this lot was his private office, a small frame building, that I remember well when a very small boy. The gentleman owning the lot lived adjoining it, and wanting it for his garden, tore down the building and turned the space into a garden-ornamental.

"The next time you come down here, I will show you both places. The latter is only two squares from Christ Church, directly east of the church."

BATH—

BATH—OR WARM SPRINGS—
Two well situated and had buildings to the amount of £150. } 800 (*w*)

(*w*) The lots in Bath (two adjoining) cost me to the best of my recollection, between fifty and sixty pounds, 20 years ago & the buildings thereon, £150 more. —Whether the property there has increased or decreased in its value, and in what condition the houses are, I am ignorant, but suppose they are not valued too high.*

---

* "Having obtained a plan of this Town (Bath), and ascertained the situation of my lots therein, which I examined; it appears that the disposition of a dwelling house, kitchen and stable, cannot be more advantageously placed than they are marked in the copy in the copy I have taken from the plan of the Town, to which I refer for recollection of my design; and Mr. Rumsey being willing to undertake those Buildings, I have agreed with him to have them finished by the 10th of next July. The dwelling House is to be 36 feet by 24, with a gallery of 7 feet on each side of the House, the whole fronts. Under the House is to be a cellar half the size of it, walled with stone, and the whole underpin'd. On the first floor are to be three rooms; one of them 24 by 20 feet, with a chimney at the end (middle thereof)—the other two to be 12 by 16 feet with corner chimneys—on the upper Floor there are to be two rooms of equal sizes, with fire places; the staircase to go up in the gallery—galleries above also. The kitchen and stable are to be of the same size—18 by 22; the first with a stone chimney and good floor above. The stable is to be sunk in the ground, so as that the floor above it on the north, or side next to the dwelling
STOCKS.

137

STOCKS.

United States 6 pr ct.　　　3,746
　　Do　　　deferred　1,873
　　　　3 pr ct.　2,946　2,500　6.246 (*x*)

(*x*) These are the sums which are actually funded, and though no more in the aggregate than $7566 stand me in at least ten thousand pounds in Virginia money, being the amount of bonded and other debts due me, and discharged during the war, when money had depreciated in that ratio ☞ and was so settled by public authority.*

House, shall be level with the Yard—to have a partition therein, the west part of which to be for a carriage, Harness, and saddles—the east for Hay or Grain. All three of the houses to be shingled with * * *. *Journal*, 1784.

*The law of 4 August, 1790, providing for the funding of the revolutionary debt called for a loan to the full amount of the debt, subscriptions to be payable in the certificates or notes issued by the Continental Congress or the respective States. For two-thirds of the subscriptions a certificate was to issue purporting that the United States owed to the holder a sum equal to such two-thirds (when paid in Continental certificates) and to two-thirds of the aforesaid two-thirds (when paid in States issues) bearing 6 per cent. interest per annum, payable quarterly, and subject to redemption by payments not exceeding 8 per cent. per annum, principal and interest. These certificates were known as the "six per cent. stock of 1790." For the balance, stock was issued not to bear interest until after 1800, when the

POTOMAC

POTOMAC COMPANY—

24 Shares cost ea £100 *Sterl'g*   10.666 (*y*)

(*y*) The value annexed to these shares is what they have actually cost me, and is the price affixed by law:—and although the present selling price is under par, my advice to the Legatees (for whose benefit they are intended, especially those who can afford to *lye* out of the money) is that each should take and hold one; there being a moral certainty of a great and increasing profit arising from them in the course of a few years.*

---

rate of six per cent. would be paid. This was the "deferred 6 per cent. stock of 1790." One-third of the amount subscribed and paid in indents of interest issued by authority of the Continental Congress, or in certificates or notes issued by the several states, should bear interest at three per cent. This was the "three per cent. stock of 1790."

* This company was organized in December, 1784, and soon after under laws of Virginia and Maryland, opened its subscription books for the sale of its 500 shares. Each state took fifty shares, and private capital soon took up the balance. Little was done towards completing the canal, and the time allowed by the legislatures was extended at the expiration of every fixed period, until 1820, when the scheme was laid aside. The tolls collected in 1800 were only $2,138, and in 1811—the most prosperous year—were $22,542. At a later period the charter was surrendered to a new company, and has never proved profitable. The State of Maryland virtually owns the canal, and since the great flood of 1889, which broke down the banks in many places, it has ceased to be a water way.

JAMES

JAMES RIVER COMPANY—
  5 Shares each cost $100 $500 (*z*)
  (*z*) It is supposed that the shares in the James River Company must also be productive—But of this I can give no decided opinion for want of more accurate information.

BANK OF COLUMBIA—
  170 shares—$40 each   6.800 ⎫
BANK OF ALEXANDRIA—besides ⎫   ⎬ (&)
  20 to the Free School 5   ⎭   1.000 ⎭

  (&) These are nominal prices of the Shares of the Bank of Alexandria & Columbia, the selling prices vary according to circumstances but as the stock usually divided from eight to ten per cent per annum, they must be worth the former, at least, so long as the Banks are conceived to be secure, although circumstances may some time [be] below it.*

STOCK—living—viz.—
  1 covering horse, 5 *Coh* horses—4 Riding do—Six brood mares—20 working horses & mares,—2 Covering Jacks & 3 young ones—10 she asses—42 working mules—15 younger ones—329 head of horned cattle—640

---
* The Bank of Alexandria, I am told, failed about the year 1831.

head

head of Sheep, and a large stock of hogs, the precise number unknown— ☛ My manager has estimated this live stock at £7,000 but I shall set it down in order to make *sd* sum at— } 15.653

Aggregate amt : $530.000

The value of live stock depends more upon the quality than quantity of the different species of it, and this again upon the demand and judgment or fancy of purchasers.

Mount Vernon,
6 *July*, 1799.   G. WASHINGTON.

At a Court held for the County of Fairfax the 20th day of January 1800, this last Will and Testament of George Washington, deceased, late President of the United States of America, was presented in Court by George Steptoe Washington, Samuel Washington, & Lawrence Lewis, three of the Executors therein named, who made oath thereto, and the same being proved by the oaths of Charles Little, Charles Simms and Ludwell Lee, to be in the true handwriting of the said Testator, as also the *Scedule* thereto annexed, and the said will, being sealed and signed by him on motion, Ordered to be Recorded—And the said Executors having given Security and performed what the Laws require,

quire, a Certificate is granted them for obtaining a probate thereof in due form.

 Teste   G. Deneale, *Cl: Fx:*
R. L. H. *fo:* Ex^d by*
 G. Deneale, *Cl: Fx:*

GEORGE WASHINGTON TO DOCTOR DAVID STUART.†

     Mount Vernon, 15 January, 1788.
Dear Sir:

In answer to your enquiries in behalf of Mr. Custis and which you requested I would commit to writing, you will please to receive and convey, the following information

---

 *"Recorded Liber H, *folio* 1, and examined." George Deneale became clerk 2d May, 1798.

 The original of this will is in the County Court House, at Fairfax Court House, Virginia, in charge of the County Clerk, Mr. F. W. Richardson. A story occasionally appears in printing, that the MS. is in the secret vaults of the British Museum, having been sold to that institution by one who obtained it during or after the civil war. The fact was, fearing lest some damage should be done to it, in July, 1861, the will was taken to Richmond by the then County Clerk, Mr. Alfred Moss, and deposited for safe keeping with the then Secretary of the Commonwealth, Mr. George W. Mumford. The office of the Secretary was looted by the Federal troops, but by some happy chance the will was thrown away, and was later found in a heap of rubbish. It was restored to the Fairfax County Court House, where it may be seen by any one who applies to the courteous Mr. Richardson.

 † As this contains the fullest account of these Western lands, I insert the letter entire.

          Namely.—

Namely.— That the lands which I have to dispose of beyond the Allegany mountains, are contained in the following tracts.

2314— Acres in Bottetourt County on the Ohio, beginning about 4 miles below the mouth of the little Kanhawa and bounded by the Ohio 1720 poles—being the first large bottom on the East side of that River, below the mouth of the little Kanhawa.

2448— Acres on the same rout and on the said river about 16 miles below the above tract, being the 4th large bottom on the east side, below the little Kanhawa.—this tract is bounded by the Ohio 1012 poles—has a fine Creek running through it which (as I am informed) [will give] Mill seats.

4395— Acres, in the same County and on the Ohio, also about 3 miles below the past mentioned tract and on the same, that is the East, side, & above the great Bend which is about 25 Miles from the mouth of the Great Kanhawa bounded by the River, 1670 poles.

In all 9.157 Acres, on the Ohio; betw^n the great and little Kanhawa.—

10.990— Acres on the Great Kanhawa, West side of it in Montgomery County,—Beginning about 2 or 3 Miles from its Conflux with the Ohio.—Bounded by the former, that is the Kanhawa, 5491 poles or 17 Miles and

51 poles. Having many valuable streams passing through it.

7276— Acres, about 2 Miles above the latter on the other or East side of the said river in Green brier County and bounded thereby. 3947 poles or 12½ Miles.

2000 Acres about 6 Miles above the last mentioned tract on the west side of River laying in the fork of the Kanhawa and Coal River—binding on the first 1400 and on the latter 588 poles.—*

2950— Acres on the east side of the Kanhawa in Green brier County part whereof is opposite to the last mentioned tract.—this is bounded by the River, 1939 poles.—

---

* "Your having mentioned that you hold land at the Mouth of Coal River, I would beg leave to observe that I have one tract of 2000 acres in the point of fork between that River and the Kanhawa running up the 1st about 2 Miles (from the point) and up the latter more than 4—and on the opposite 2 miles above the fork another of my tracts for 3000 Acres begins, and runs upwards 6 Miles bordering on the River for quantity. As these tracts are in the vicinity of yours it is possible you may have been on them in which case I would thank you for your opinion of them—From the mouth of Pohitelleca on the East Side the River for 13 miles down the Kanhawa I hold the land —and on the other side, from within 2 or 3 miles of the mouth I have a tract which runs near 20 Miles along the River equal to any and I have ever seen, all of which may be Seated as hath been mentioned, together with that on the Ohio above."
Washington to Henry Banks, 22 November, 1787.

In

In all 23216   Acres on the Great Kanhawa.—and 9.157 on the Ohio—on both Rivers.—

Total.32.373

That these several tracts, *some* from my own observation, and *all* from good information, are of the richest low grounds; being the first choice of the Country, by a competent Judge, and are well watered and superabounding in fine meadow.

That the whole are to be let, on the Conditions hereafter mentioned.

That the two first mentioned on the Ohio—and the two last named on the Kanhawa may be purchased—as indeed all of them may if any one person for himself, or in behalf of a number, will strike for the whole—without this, and not because they are of inferior quality, but because what remains will be more concentered, I incline to sell those that are farthest apart first.

That if I sell these, I shall expect (considering the quality of the soil, there situations on navigable waters; and the advantages they possess on account of Fish wild fowl, &c.) Twenty Shillings p^r Acre.—part of the monies to be paid down, and such credit as can be agreed upon given for the residue. I have been in treaty with some foreigners (thro' there agent Mr Charson) who have large tracts of land, back of or in the vicinity of some of these Lands of mine, and who know them perfectly well, for the whole of them at the price of 30,000 guineas—but as they are not yet returned

turned from Europe and the time is elapsed in which they were to have given me a definitive answer, I do not consider myself bound any longer to them, tho' it has been the cause (in a great measure) of the lands remaining unsold.

That the enclosed Gazette will explain *my* ideas of what I conceive the Rents *ought* to be.—but as this, it seems, is not the mode which is practiced by, and most agreeable to, the people in that Country possible from the scarcity of money or want hitherto must conform to the custome of it and of established markets.

I have accordingly within the course of the last month authorized Col. Thomas Lewis who lives (at Point Pleasant, a town at the mouth of the Great Kanhawa in which I am told 30 or 40 families are settled and which lies in the center between my several tracts, to let them on the following terms that is to say.—

First. With an exemption from the payment of rent 3 years, provided in that time a reasonable quantity of land is cleared and cultivated ; a comfortable House, or houses for the accommodation of a family is built and a reasonable number of frute trees planted.—And provided also (if it be customary) that the Land tax of whatever the tenant may be inclined to hold is paid by them.

Second. That after the expiration of the third year Rents shall commence and, as the custom of the Country, is to be received in the specific articles that are raised on the tenement, and in the proportion of one third, by my Collector, or agent being near the premises.

Third.

Third. That under this tenure the tenant may have a certainty of holding their places (if they incline to remain and will continue to improve them) for a certain number of years (but not for lives) which may be agreed upon.

Fourth. That all mines and minerals, with free egress and regress, shall be reserved.—and an extra allowance made for Mill Seats, or a reservation of them if there is not.

Altho' in the hands of Industrious tenants and a good & faithful Collector, Rents paid in this manner and proportion would far exceed what I have required in my printed proposals, yet I must confess that it is not a pleasing thing to me to let them on these terms because there is no certainty in the revenue which will arise from it. Idle tenants will pay little—dishonest ones will cheat me—and an indolent, or speculating Collector will make poor returns. Otherwise as I have already observed no money rents that can be fixed would be so productive. For instance suppose a farm of 100 Acres (which of such land is enough for any man who has only a wife and their children to assist him) and ten only of these for the land is most easily cleared, is in cultivation, Corn we will say, at the expiration of the 3^d year—this it is agreed *on all hands*, will yield 60 to 100 Bushels to the acre—but call it 50 only, it makes 500 Bushels the $\frac{1}{3}$ of which is 166 bushels—the demand for which in a Country whose population is encreasing every year by thousands of emegrants will hardly ever let this article be under a Shilling; but was it not more than *half* which is scarcely within the bounds

bounds of possibility, it would amount to £4. 3 P. Hundred Acres.

If Mr. Custis, or his neighbours of whom you made mention to me has any inclination buy or rent any of my Lands here described. It would not be improper to suggest to them that the sooner something is resolved on the better: for as well formerly as lately, it has been told me, that I may soon fill my lands, with tenants agreeably to the terms on which Col? Lewis has been empower'd to grant them; and on which if nothing more pleasing to *both* parties can be agreed, M! Custis's neighbours may have them.

Should these circumstances, & conditions on which I have offered to sell part or Rent the whole of these lands induce M! Custis to take a trip by water, or land, to this place, I will shew him the plats of several tracts, the manner in which the land lays, give him a more ample description of the advantages which attends it, and if any terms can be agreed upon between us will endeavor in time to prevent the seating of them by Col? Lewis, by whose agreements I must be bound, if he makes any, as I have given him full powers to let the Land.—

I am, &c—

G? WASHINGTON.

WILL

OF

BUSHROD WASHINGTON,

NEPHEW OF

GEORGE WASHINGTON.

In the name of God amen. I Bushrod Washington, of Mount Vernon, do make this my last will and testament hereby revoking all former wills by me made.

Imprimis. I give to my dear and most excellent wife,* and her heirs the following negroes, viz. Ann Luisa, & the children she now has, or may hereafter have, Sam, Jessy, Clark and Silvia his wife and Lucy their daughter, with all the future increase of the females, and also Jenny who I purchased from Mr. Turner.

Second. I give to my said wife during her life, the whole of my Mt. Vernon land, except such parts thereof as will be hereafter given in trust for my nephew, Bushrod Washington, and also all the rest of my negroes of which I may die possessed or entitled to.

Third. I give to my said wife during her life the interest which may accrue after my death upon the debts now due or which may hereafter become due to me, as well as the dividends & interest which may accrue and to be declared upon my bank and road stock, upon my share in the Dismal Swamp

---

*Ann, daughter of Col. Thomas Blackburn, of Rippon Lodge, Prince William county. She survived her husband but a few days, and died without issue.

Land Company, and all other stocks to which I may be entitled at the time of my death. I also give to her during her life the whole of my household and kitchen furniture, liquors so much thereof as she may require for the use of her Family, riding carriages, horses, mules, cattle, sheep, hogs, plantation utensils, waggons, & carts on hand & provisions laid in for the use of my family at the time of my death, or fattening at that time for such use. The use only of the above articles is intended to be given to my said wife during her life.

Fourth. It is my will that as soon & as fast as the debts to me are collected, their amount, including whatever I may be entitled to receive from the estate of my deceased uncle General George Washington, in my own right or as an assignee of Major Geo. Lewis, & on account of my commissions as Executor, and all rents due to me at the time of my death may be invested by my Executors in publick or other safe stocks, the interest whereof may accrue during the life of my wife I give to her.

Fifth. I give to my said wife all the furniture of her chamber, also the organ and pianos, books of music and her Library of books kept by herself separate from mine, her Jewels and paraphernalia of every kind. And whereas there are certain prints hanging in some of the rooms which I have given and now confirm to my said wife, but which I cannot now describe, it is my will that she shall
have

have such of them as she may by some writing under her hand, attested by one witness at least, and delivered during her life to one of my Executors, distinctly point and describe. Unless my wife should dispose of the organ by will or by some other act during her life, I give the same to the person to whom I shall hereafter devise the mansion house, as it would hardly suit any other room than that in which it now stands.

Sixth. After the death of my said wife, I give to my nephew John A. Washington and to his heirs all that part of my Mount Vernon Land included within the following boundaries, to wit:

Beginning at the Gum Spring on or near the line between Mr. Peake & myself and running thence the straight road along where the post and rail fence, ran to the gate leading into the house, & pursuing the road passing the said Gate leading to the old Ferry house occupied lately by James Dorsey till it comes to the corner of the fence on the road leading to the union farm barn, & thence along the fence and road leading to said barn to the first wattle fence made by Ja: Dorsey, (at which point it is my intention to put down a post) and then along said wattle fence, rectangular or nearly so, to the last line to the creek, and so with the meanders of said creek, the river and hunting creek, including the fisheries and marshes to the beginning. I also give to my said nephew John,
after

after the death of my said wife, all the green house and hot house plants and tools or instruments belonging to the gardens, & also give to my said nephew after the death of my said wife all the furniture belonging, and which at the time of my death may belong to, and be in the mansion house, kitchen, & other houses (not before given to my wife,) in which bequest to avoid disputes, I mean to include not only the standing furniture, but also the silver and plated ware, cut and other glass, pictures, prints, Table & bed furniture, & in short every thing used and generally considered as furniture. All the Liquors of every kind remaining in the house at the death of my wife unused by her, I give to be equally divided between my nephews, Bushrod Washington, of Mt. Zephire,* Geo. C. Washington,† John A. Washington,‡ and Bushrod C. Washington.§

---

* Son of William Augustine Washington and Jane, his cousin, a daughter of John Augustine Washington. Bushrod was born 4 April, 1785, and was settled at Mt. Zephyr, Virginia. Married Henrietta, daughter of General Alexander Spotswood, and died in 1830.

† Also a son of William Augustine Washington, born 20 August, 1789, married in 1807 Eliza Ridgeley Beall, and died in Georgetown, 17 July, 1854.

‡ Son of Corbin Washington and Hannah Lee, daughter of Richard Henry Lee. He married Jane Charlotte Blackburn.

§ Also son of Corbin Washington. He removed to Claymont, Jefferson County, [West] Virginia, and died there in 1851. He married (1) Anna Maria Blackburn, and (2) Maria Powell Harrison.

Seventh.

Seventh. After the death of my wife I give to my dear niece Mary Lee Herbert,* & her heirs, all that part of my Mount Vernon Tract of Land, beginning at the Knowl opposite to the old road, which formerly passed through the lower field of Muddy hole farm, at which, on the north side of said road, are or were three red or Spanish oaks, marked as a corner, (which spot is mentioned in the Will of General Washington,) thence rectangular by a line of trees to the back line or outer boundary of the tract between General Thomson Mason, (now in possession of his son,) and myself, thence with that line Easterly along the double ditch to the run of Little Hunting creek, thence with that run to the gum spring, thence along the most northerly of the two roads being that leading to Major Lewis' mill, to the beginning.

Eighth. I give to my nephew George C. Washington, and his heirs, on my death, all the land from the Gum Spring aforesaid lying between the road leading to Mt. Vernon until it comes to the lower end or corner of the field (N? 3) in the plot made by Gen'l Washington, amongst my Mount Vernon Land papers,† by James Nugent's quarter, that was, & the road leading from the said Gum

---

* Mary Lee Washington, daughter of Corbin Washington, married Noblet Herbert in 1819.

† This survey is now in the possession of Dr. Thomas Addis Emmet, of New York.

spring

spring to Major Lewis' mill 'till it comes to the inner and upper corner of my new ground 216 acre field, & thence with the inner fence of the said new ground field dividing the same from the Mt. Zephyr land, to the lower end or corner of the said inner fence near the spring, thence easterly along the lower fence of Bushrod Washington Jr's new ground, as it now runs and crosses the swamp 'till it comes to the edge of the woods on the easterly side of the swamp to an old road, & thence with said old road & along the edge of the woods to the lower fence of the said Bushrod Washington Jr's meadow, below his house, and thence easterly following the fence as it now runs to the road at James Nugent's where there is a gate, which said lines enclose the whole of the cleared land now in possession of the said Bushrod Washington, Jr. Also a small part of the swamp on the east side of the ditch to the edge of the woods, and also a small angle of wood land lying between the aforesaid two roads in which stood the school house. I also give to the said Geo. C. Washington in fee one half of the aforesaid new ground field, being that half which lies to the northward of the red line run from the corner of the fence before mentioned, near the spring before mentioned, called A in S^m Summer's plot & survey of the said new ground field to B, which half in the said plot is marked N° 2, as by reference to said plat and survey, dated July, 1813, amongst

amongst the Mount Vernon Land papers will more fully appear. I also give to the said Geo. C. Washington & his heirs, one equal half part of the wood land adjoining the afs^d clear land to be laid off by a line running from the road leading from the Gum spring to the porter's lodges, north westerly to the old road by the swamp & edge of the woods before mentioned in this clause, the said division to be according to the quantity. The other half of the wood land here intended, extending to the road leading from the porter's lodge to the union farm gate, being contiguous to that part of the Estate, will be disposed of by a future clause of this will to the person to whom that part of the land will be devised. If any disagreements should arise respecting the lines of division mentioned in this Will, it is my desire that the parties concerned should submit the same to arbitration, and I declare that all the lands mentioned in this clause and devised to the said Geo. C. Washington, are given in trust to permit my nephew Bushrod Washington, Jr. his Brother, to receive the rents, issues and profits there of during his life, and after his death then in trust for the children of the said Bushrod Washington, living at his death & their heirs, equally to be divided.

Ninth. All the rest and residue of my Mt. Vernon estate not before disposed of, I give, after the death of my wife to be equally divided between my
nephews

nephews George C. Washington & Bushrod C. Washington and their heirs.

Tenth. I give my Ohio tract of land immediately on my death as follows, one equal fifth part to my nephew Geo. C. Washington, and his heirs, one other fifth part to my niece Mary L. Herbert and her heirs, one other fifth part to the said Geo. [C.] Washington, and his heirs to the same uses and under the same limitations as are mentioned in the 8th clause aforesaid, in respect to the part of the Mt. Vernon Land devised to him in trust, and the other two fifths I give to my nephews Jno. A. Washington & Bushrod C. Washington and their heirs equally to be divided : Should the said Geo. C. Washington, think it most to the advantage of the said Bushrod Washington, Jr. to sell the part of the Ohio land hereby devised to him, in trust, he may do the same at public or private sale, on such terms as he may think best, the proceeds to be invested in some productive fund & the interest or dividends to be paid to the said Bushrod Washington Jr. during his life, and after his death to be equally divided between the children of the said Bushrod Washington Jr. who shall be living at his death, their heir and assigns.

Eleventh. I desire that all my law books in Philadelphia and a few others left with Mr. Berkham in Trenton may be removed to Mt. Vernon, and together with those now there may remain in the

the study under the care of Jno. A. Washington, until Bushrod Washington Herbert, son of my niece aforesaid, arrives to the age of 21, & in case he should be educated & prepared to practice law I give all the said books to him; But if, at the above period he should not be destined to the bar, or in case of his death before the said age, I desire the said books may be sold and the proceeds to sink into the residuum of my Estate. Wheaton's Reports belong to the United States and are to be delivered to the person authorized to receive them.

Twelfth. After the death of my wife, I give all the rest and residue of my Estate real and personal in possession or expectancy and not by this will otherwise disposed of as follows: viz: one fifth part to my nephew Geo. C. Washington & his heirs, one other fifth part to John A. Washington, my nephew and his heirs, one other fifth part to his brother Bushrod C. Washington and his heirs, another fifth part to my niece Mary L. Herbert, & her heirs, & the remaining fifth part to the said Geo. C. Washington & his heirs in trust for the same uses & under the same limitations as are mentioned in the eighth clause of this will in respect to the part of the Mt. Vernon land devised to him in trust for Bushrod Washington, Jr. & his children. It is further my will that my nephew John A. Washington may be at liberty

erty after my wife's death to take the Gardner Phil at his appraised value to be paid my Executors.

Thirteenth: All the papers and letter books devised to me by my uncle Gen'l Washington, as well as the books in my study, other than law books, I give to my nephew Geo. C. Washington; the books in the cases in the dining room, I give to my nephew John A. Washington.

Fourteenth: The sword left to me by Genl. Washington, I give to the aforesaid Geo. C. Washington under the same injunctions that it was bestowed to me. My gold watch I give to my friend Robert Adams, of Philadelphia, knowing that he will appreciate the gift not for the intrinsic value of the article but because it was worn by the father of his country and afterwards by his friend: After the death of the said Robt. Adams, I give the said watch to his son Bushrod. I give Cooke's Edition of Hogarth with the key, to my nephew John, and Alexander's victories to my nephew Bush: C. Washington.* I also give to my said nephew John, the two Globes & the busts of Gen'l Washington†

---

* In the New York Exhibition 1889, were shown by Bushrod C. Washington some old line engravings by P. Ganst, from the original painting by Le Bruu, victories of Alexander the Great. "The pictures are supposed to have been given to General Washington by Lafayette" *Catalogue.*

† By Houdon.

& Neckar.

& Neckar.* The bust of Paul Jones I give to Mr. Mumford for his museum. My double barrel gun I give to my nephew Bushrod Washington Jr. and the pistols which belonged to & were used by Gen'l Washington, to Geo. C. Washington. Watts' views I give to my highly valued friend Mr. Justice Story.

Fifteenth. The debts due me from the Estates of my deceased friends Major Richard Blackburn & Thomas Blackburn, I hereby forgive and release.

Sixteenth. I give to West Ford the tract of land on Hunting creek adjoining Mr. Geo. Mason and that occupied by Dr. Peake, which I purchased from Noblet Herbert deceased, which was conveyed to him by Francis Adams, to him the said West Ford, & his heirs. Whatever appears by my Ledger to be due to said West Ford is to be paid to him, & it is my request that he will continue in his present situation and employment during the

---

*This bust was sold at auction in Philadelphia, April 1891. On the pedestal were two brass plates, on the lower of which was engraved

PRESENTED TO
GEORGE WASHINGTON
PRESIDENT OF THE UNITED STATES OF AMERICA
BY HIS MOST DUTIFUL, MOST OBEDIENT, AND MOST HUMBLE
servant, ESTAING, A CITIZEN OF THE STATE OF
GEORGIA, BY AN ACT OF THE 22ND FEBRUARY, 1785,
AND A CITIZEN OF FRANCE IN 1786.

life

life of my wife provided she wishes him to do so on the terms he is now living with me.*

Seventeenth. Whereas, as Trustee for the creditors of my nephew Bushrod Washington Jr., I have made advances greatly beyond the value of the property conveyed to me, besides being a considerable creditor of my said nephew, & entitled to come in as such under the deed of trust, & whereas the unsold trust property, that is to say the following negroes, Nat, Sue, Isaac, Joshua, Tetia & her 7 children, James, William, Nancy, John, Henry, Betsy, & Judy. Also Eliza, and her two children Warren & Geo. Also Nanny, who have this day been valued by Lawrence Lewis and Saml. Collard at the price of $2205, fall very short of the amount due to me from the said trust estate and for which the said property is answerable, I do hereby give the said negroes and the future increase of the females to my aforesaid nephew Geo. C. Washington & his heirs upon the trusts and under the same limitations as are mentioned in the 8th clause of this will in respect to the part of the Mt. Vernon land devised to him in trust. I also give and release to my said nephew Bushrod Washington, Jr., all and every sum and sums of money due by him to me, and which yet remain unsatisfied.

Lastly. I nominate and appoint my nephews

---

* West Ford was a mulatto house servant. His portrait is given by Lossing in his *Home of Washington*.

John

John A. Washington & Bushrod C. Washington my Executors, who are to give no security for the discharge of their duties. In witness whereof, I have hereunto set my hand and affixed my seal, having written the whole of this will with my own hand, this 10th day July 1826.

BUSH: WASHINGTON, [SEAL.]

Memorandum. All the erasures & interlineations in this will have been made with my own hand.

B. W.

This is a codicil to my will written and dated this 10th day of July, 1826.

Whereas Chief Justice Marshall & myself contemplate publishing some volumes of letters from Genl. Washington all or the most of which are already copied & also publishing a second edition of the life of Washington, it is my will that whatever sum of money may accrue from these sources be invested by my executor in some productive fund, the interest or dividends whereof are to be paid to my wife during her life and after her death to be divided and to vest in the persons to whom the residue of my Estate is given to and for the same uses and under the same limitations.

Item. I give to our niece Jane C. Washington, wife of my nephew John A. Washington, & to her heirs a negro boy called Lewis, son of Ozman & Aggy.

Item.

Item. And whereas it may so happen that my wife may die without making any disposition of the property, I have devised to her in fee simple, I give to her niece Jane C. Washington, in that event, and that only the organ and piano forte, together with all the musick, also all the books in the chamber book cases and chamber closet, also the chamber furniture and the prints mentioned in my will. All the rest of the property so devised to my wife, I give, in the said event, to be equally divided between such of the nieces of my said wife as may be living at the time of her death. The property which I have purchased from the Executors of Nob: Herbert dec^d ; and from the Administrators of Richard H. L. Washington, dec^d, & which I have conveyed to my niece, Mary L. Herbert, for whom I bought the whole, and have given her possession, I hereby confirm and ratify.

In witness whereof, I have here unto set my hand and affixed my seal this 10th day of July, 1826, the whole of this codicil being written with my own hand & all erasures & interlineations in the will and codicil being made by myself before they were signed and sealed.

BUSH: WASHINGTON. [SEAL.]

This is a second codicil to my will. Imprimis, my beloved niece Mary L. Herbert having died since the making of my former will, I here by give and

and bequeath all the property real and personal in possession or expectancy devised to her to be equally divided between her two sons Bushrod W. Herbert and Noblet Herbert and their heirs, & in the case of the death of either with out child or children, his part to go to the survivor, & in case of the death of both without child or children, the whole then remaining I give to be divided amongst my four nephews & their heirs, the part of my nephew Bushrod under the same trust and to the same trustee as are mentioned in the 8th Clause of my will: all the personal property except negroes, now in possession of my said nephew Bushrod Washington on hire I give to him. Item. If Bushrod W. Herbert should not practice law, I give my law library to such of the sons of my nephew John A. Washington as may practice it, & if more than one should, then to the eldest, and if neither should, then the same is to be sold and the proceeds disposed of as directed by the eleventh clause of my will. Item. Having subscribed for 50 shares, in the Chesapeake & Ohio Canal which I trust may be paid for without a sale of other property, I hereby appropriate for that purpose, whatever ready money I may have in any bank or banks at my death, & whatever salary may be due to me at that time, & I further empower my Executor to apply to the same purpose so much of the income of my Estate, or monies he may collect,

lect, as may remain after amply supplying the wants of my dear wife, to whom I hereby give during her life the dividends which may arise on said canal stock. But if these funds should be insufficient to comply with the calls of the company, my said Executors may sell as much of my bank stock as may be sufficient. In witness whereof I have hereunto set my hand & affix my seal the 19th day of January 1828, the whole of this codicil being written with my own hand & all erasures and interlineations being made by myself before signing and sealing this codicil.

    BUSH: WASHINGTON [SEAL.]

 This is a third codicil to my will.

Whereas the line between Major Lewis & myself from the three red or Spanish oaks marked as a corner and a stone placed, thence by a line of trees to be marked rectangular to the back line or outer boundary of the tract between Thomson Mason & Genl. Washington, as described in the clause of Genl. Washington's will, which devises a part of the Mount Vernon estate to me, has never been run by the major and myself, and there subsists a difficulty of opinion between us to the construction of the said will in relation to that line which my frequent and long absences from home have hitherto prevented us from adjusting, it is my will that my nephews, the Executors and Trustees of of my deceased niece Mary L. Herbert, (in case it should not be in my power to settle this matter with Major Lewis, during my life,) do as soon as possible settle and adjust with him this controverted line & in order that it may be done in the most amicable manner, I do hereby empower my said nephews John A. and Bushrod C. Washington, or either of them, or the survivor of them, to submit any disputed point relative to that subject to arbitration hereby declaring any award or awards to be made in the premises to be final and binding on the persons who may be entitled to that part of the land devised by the preceding codicil to the sons of my niece Mary L. Herbert in like manner as it would were the submission made by me during my life.

Item. I give the interest which after my death may become due on Geo. Atkinson's bond until George W. Washington, son of Bushrod Washington, of Mt. Zephyr, shall arrive at the age of 18 (and which my Executor is to collect as it becomes due), to be divided as follows: viz.: one third to Ann Eliza, one third to Jane Mildred, daughters of the said Bushrod Washington, Jr. of Mt. Zephyr, & the other third to the before mentioned Geo. W. son of the said Bushrod Washington Jr., towards his education & fitting him for the navy, & after he has arrived at the age of 18, then I give the whole of the said debt principal & interest, with all the securities for the same to be equally divided
between

between the said Ann Eliza and Jane Mildred Washington, & their assigns. The above bequest is intended to be made to my Executors in strict trust for the uses above mentioned & the principal to be paid to my nieces on their respective marriages and not before.

Item. It is my wish that my Executor may add to the above bequest to the said Geo. W. as much out of the income of my Estate as will complete his Education till his arrival at the age aforesaid, if in his Judgment the same can be spared after paying up my subscription to the Chesapeake & Ohio canal company, & any other debts, and providing for the comfortable and abundant support of my dear wife. All benefit under this clause in favor of the said Geo. W. to cease after he arrives at the af^{sd} age, except a moderate outfit which is to be given him in case he should be received as a midshipman in our navy. In witness whereof I have hereunto set my hand & affixed my seal this 19th day of July, 1828, the whole of this codicil being written with my own hand, & all erasures & interlineations being made by myself before signing & sealing the same.

BUSH: WASHINGTON.

At a Court held for Fairfax county, the 21st. day of December, 1829.

This last will & testament of the Honorable Bushrod

Bushrod Washington, of Mt. Vernon, deceased, together with three Codicils thereto annexed, was presented in Court by Jno. A. Washington, one of the Executors therein named, & the same being proved to be wholly in the handwriting of the said Bushrod Washington by the oaths of Geo. Mason, Geo. Millan, Dennis Johnson, & Wm. Moss, is admitted to record. And the said John A. Washington having in open court executed bond in the penalty of $100,000 conditioned as the law directs, & taken the oath prescribed by law, a certificate is granted him for obtaining a probate thereof in due form.

Teste

WM. MOSS, C. C.

A true copy.
  Teste:
    F. W. RICHARDSON,
      Deputy Clerk.
        21 November, 1878.

WILL

OF

JOHN AUGUSTINE WASHINGTON.

In the name of God amen. I John A. Washington, of Jefferson county, in the State of Virginia, being in perfect health of body & of sound and disposing mind, memory and understanding, considering the certainty of death & the uncertainty of the time thereof & being desirous to settle my worldly affairs, & therefore be the better prepared to leave this world, when it shall please God to call me hence, do therefore make this my last will and testament, in manner and form following, that is to say. First. It is my will & desire that all my just debts and funeral charges be paid & discharged as soon as possible, by my Executrix here in after mentioned.

Secondly. I give & bequeath unto my most dear wife & friend Jane C. Washington,* all my negroes and other real & personal Estate of every kind and description whatsoever, that I now have or may here after have any right to dispose of by will or otherwise in possession, to hold during her widowhood.

Thirdly. I do hereby fully empower my dear wife Jane C. Washington, to divide my said Estate among my children in any way she may think proper.

---

*Daughter of Richard Scott Blackburn.

Fourthly.

Fourthly. As it frequently happens that negroes become extremely disobedient to their mistress after the death of their masters, I do hereby give my said dear wife full power & authority should any act so unfaithfully to her orders, to sell and dispose of any of them so offending in her opinion, & vest the money arising there from, in other negroes, property or public stock, which at the death of my dear wife Jane C. Washington is to be divided between my children as she may direct.

Fifthly. It is my will & desire that my Executrix shall not be compelled to give security upon qualifying to my will, and that she may not be put to the trouble of having the Estate appraised. Also I do hereby appoint her sole Guardian to all my children, without giving security for the same.

Lastly. I do hereby constitute & appoint my most dear & affectionate wife Jane C. Washington my sole Executrix to this my last will & testament, revoking & annulling all former wills by me heretofore made ratifying and confirming this and none other to be my last will & testament. In testimony where of I have hereunto set my hand and affixed my seal, in my own handwriting, this 6th. day of August 1822. The erasures in lines 7 & 8, on page second, I did myself before I set my hand and affixed my seal.

    JOHN A. WASHINGTON. [SEAL.]

Codicil—Whereas I, John A. Washington, in the County

County of Jefferson, & State of Virginia, have
made & duly executed my last will and testament
in writing, bearing date as above, which said last
will & testament, & every clause, bequest and devise therein contained, I do hereby ratify and confirm & being desirous to alter some parts thereof,
provided my dear wife Jane C. Washington should
die without making her last will devising my estate
as she may think proper between my children, in
that case only do I therefore hereby make this my
codicil, which I will & direct shall be taken & held
as my will & testament in manner as following :
that is to say, I hereby give & devise all my negroes & other personal & real Estate of every kind
& description whatsoever that I now have or may
hereafter have any right to dispose of by will or
otherwise, in possession, reversion or remainder, to
my sons and to their heirs forever in equal proportions to be allotted to each of them as soon as they
arrive at the age of 21 years, except what I shall
hereafter devise. I do hereby declare that should
either of my sons die without lawful issue the
property so descending shall go to the surviving
brother or brothers. Item. I give & bequeath to
my dear daughter Anne Maria Washington ten
thousand dollars current money of the United
States to bear interest from the death of my wife
Jane C. Washington, to be raised in the most convenient manner to the Estate, as speedily as possible

sible after her decease ; a negro man and woman, not to exceed 25 years of age, also a good riding horse, saddle & bridle, to be paid to her when she arrives at the age of 21 years or marries. In testimony where of I have hereunto set my hand & affixed my seal, in my own handwriting, this 10th day of September, 1822, the erasure in lines 7 & 8 on page second I did myself before I set my hand & affixed my seal.

   JOHN A. WASHINGTON. [SEAL.]

 Codicil 2d. Whereas my late uncle Bushrod Washington did by will give to me the Mount Vernon house and a certain parcel of land attached thereto, I do hereby authorize my Executrix or Administrator should they deem it advisable for my children's interest to sell to the Government of the United States only if they should be disposed to purchase Mount Vernon & as much of the land as they may want, the proceeds to be laid out in public stock for the benefit of my children. If the Congress of the United States will take Mt. Vernon & part of the land, my Executrix or Administrator may sell the balance to any person or persons, also all undivided property received from the said Bushrod Washington & the amount laid out in public stock for the benefit of my children. In testimony whereof, I have hereunto set my hand & affixed my seal, in my own hand writing this
           Eighth

Eighth day of July in the year of our Lord one thousand eight hundred & thirty.*

JOHN A. WASHINGTON. [SEAL.]

STATE OF VIRGINIA } ss.
COUNTY OF JEFFERSON

In the county court, July term, 1832.

At a court held for the said county on the 16th day of July, 1832. The last will and testament of John A. Washington dec. is this day proved in open court by the oaths of Bushrod C. Washington and Edmund I. Lee, Junr, to be altogether in the handwriting of the said testator, & ordered to be recorded, & on the same day on motion of Mrs. Jane C. Washington, the executrix named in the said will, who made oath according to law, & entered into and acknowledged a bond without security, in the penalty of $50,000 with condition according to law, the said testator having directed that no security should be required of her, certifi-

---

* In 1847 John A. Washington offered to sell Mount Vernon to the United States government for $100,000, under certain conditions, one of which was that in the event of a dissolution of the existing federal government, the property should revert to the Washington heirs. The offer was not accepted, and in 1855, under the lead of Mrs. Ann Pamelia Cunningham, the Mount Vernon Ladies' Association was formed to purchase the house and two hundred acres of the estate. Its efforts to raise the sum needed, $200,000, were successful, and since that time the property has been under their care, much improved, and many scattered relics brought together.

cate

cate is granted her for obtaining letters testamentary in due form.

Teste:
SAMUEL J. CRANE, Clerk.

And afterwards, to wit: At a Court held for the said County on the 16th day of July 1849. It appearing to the satisfaction of the Court, that in making the entry of the proof of the last will & testament of John A. Washington, deceased, at July Term, 1832, of this Court, it was proved that both will & codicils were in the hand writing of the Testator, & that the record inadvertently mentions that the will had been proved omitting the codicils, on motion leave is given to examine the same witnesses again, which being done & it being proved by the said witnesses Bushrod C. Washington & Edmund I. Lee, that the said will & codicils are all in the hand writing of the said John A. Washington, the said testator, the same is ordered to be entered on record, which is accordingly hereby done.

Teste:
T. A. MOORE, Clerk.

And at a Court held for the said county on the 12th day of Octo. 1857. On motion of Richard B. Washington* who made oath according to law &

---

* Youngest son of John Augustine Washington. The other children were George, Ann Maria, John Augustine and a daughter, who died young.

with

with Robt. W. Baylor his security, entered into and acknowledged a Bond in the penalty of $5,000 with condition according to law, certificate is granted him for obtaining letters of administration *de bonis non*, with the will annexed of John A. Washington, deceased, in due form (the Executrix who heretofore qualified having departed this life).*

Teste:
T. A. Moore, Clerk.

True copy.
  Teste:
    T. A. Moore, Clerk.

---

* Died at Blakeley, Jefferson county, in August, 1856.

WILL

OF

JOHN CUSTIS.

IN THE NAME OF GOD AMEN I John Custis Esq? of Northampton County in Virginia being at present in perfect Health and sound in memory, thanks be to the Almighty, but considering the State of Mankind, how soon they are taken out of this life, and being willing to settle those Worldly Goods, God of his infinite mercy and goodness far beyond my deserts, he hath bestowed upon me do make, ordain, and appoint this my last Will and Testament, revoking all former Wills and Deeds of Gift whatever.

IMPRIMIS I give my Soul to God, that gave it me, my Body I give to the Earth from whence it came, to have a decent Burial at the discretion of my executors hereafter named, no ways doubting through the Mercy and merits of my dear Saviour Christ Jesus to have a joyful resurrection.

ITEM My Will and desire is, that my dear and loving Wife Sarah Custis live during pleasure at my now dwelling House, and Plantation at Hungars not to be disturbed by any pretence whatever while she liveth, but if it please God she marries, her Husband immediately enter into Bond with Security to keep all the Housing, fencing, and Plantation in good repair, and in Case of failure my son Hancock Custis, or his heirs enter into

the

the said Houses and Plantation the Bond to be made to Hancock Custis, or his heirs, in the sum of five hundred pounds sterling.

ITEM My will and desire is, that my dear Wife Sarah Custis have besides what I shall hereafter give her the feather Bed and Furniture we usely lye on, one pair of good Sheets, one pair of Blankets, her choice of all my riding Horses with her riding furniture with her choice of any copper kettle she please.

ITEM I Give and bequeath unto my said dear Wife all the Negroes & Slaves of what sort soever, that I had with her, I likewise give her my Mulattoe Woman Chocolate with all her increase that she now hath or shall have, my Negro men named Peter, and Trout, and my Girl Dennis to her, and her heirs forever.

ITEM I lend to my said Wife during her Widowhood, my Negro man called Michael, my Indian Woman called Sarah, and my Mulattoe Girl called Emmanuel. But in case of my said Wife's Death or marriage, then the said Slaves to return to those that I shall hereafter give them to, in this Will, and my Negro man Bristol during her Widowhood, this with my hand.

ITEM my Will and desire is, that what goods, Household Stuff, Cattle and Sheep, I have hereafter given to my Children, the like proportionable part shall be set apart for my now Wife, before the rest of of my Estate be divided, the particulars of which, I shall hereafter insert.

ITEM I give and bequeath to my son John Custis my Chiconessex Plantation with all the Stock that shall be found thereon of what nature soever to him and his heirs forever. I likewise give to my said son Arlington House together with two hundred and fifty acres of Land thereto belonging which I bought of Mr. William Willett, and have Patent for it, in my own name with the Appurtenances thereto belonging to him and his heirs forever.

ITEM I give and bequeath unto my said son all my Stock of Male cattle, that he found upon Smiths Insland and Mackean Island after my decease. I say Male Cattle with my own hand.

ITEM I likewise give and bequeath unto my said son one large Silver Dish, six large Silver Plates, one large Silver Bason, two Silver Candlesticks, with a Silver Snuff Dish, and two Silver Snuffers, one good feather Bed, and furniture, and the second choice of my riding Horses, my best Saddle and furniture, and his choice of my Cases of Pistols, and Holsters, and my best sword to him and his heirs forever.

ITEM I give and bequeath unto my son Hancock Custis after my dear Wife's decease or relinquishment, my now dwelling House & Plantation containing fifteen hundred Acres of Land with
all

all the Appurtenances thereunto belonging during his natural life together with that Tract of Land, I bought of Captain Isaac Foxcraft containing by estimation three hundred and forty Acres of Land (be the same, more or less) commonly called and known by the Davis, with that land I bought of Pierce Davis, which makes upon that quantity, and after his decease, to the heir of his Body lawfully begotten (That is to say) it is my true intent and meaning, that my said son hath power to divide the said Land between two of his issue male, How and what quantity he shall think fit, and they to enjoy it, and their heirs forever. But if it should happen that my said son should dye, without heir male, then I give it to his heirs female, and their Heirs forever, but for want of such heir to my heir at common Law forever.

ITEM I Give and bequeath unto my said son Hancock Custis, and his heirs forever, my Plantation in Accomack County, containing by estimation two thousand acres of Land, together with three hundred Acres of Swamp low Land lying near the Land, I sold to William Bradwater, which I have reserved for timber for the supply of the two thousand Acres of Land which I Give to my said son, and his heirs forever. But it is my Will and desire that my now wife Sarah Custis have free liberty of range for twenty Steers during her natural life. All the rest of my Land lying at Pocomock

comock that I shall not be disposed of, in my lifetime, I Give and bequeath to my son John Custis, and his heirs and assigns forever.

ITEM I Give and bequeath unto my son Hancock Custis besides what already I have given him, these following Negros & Slaves (viz.) Simon, Dum, Harry, Bristol, Michael, and Emmanuel always excepted, that my Wife have the use of the said Michael and Emmanuel as before excepted in my will:—and Bristol.

ITEM I Give and bequeath unto my son Henry Custis five hundred & fifty acres of Land on Jingoteague Island which I had of Captain William Kendall* together with an Island adjoining thereto by a Bridge commonly called and known by the name of Wild Cat Island by estimation two hundred and fifty acres of Land with all Marshes and other advantages thereto belonging to him the said Henry Custis, and his heir and assigns forever: Always Provided, and it is my will and desire that my now Wife have liberty of range for twenty steers upon the said Island during her natural life, with free liberty of bringing of and carrying on at her pleasure.

ITEM I Give and bequeath unto my said son

---

*In Palmer's *Calendar of State Papers* is printed a reply of the Onondagos to the propositions of Col. William Kendall, "Agent for ye Country of Virginia," 1679.

Henry

Henry Custis these following Negros and Slaves (viz) Daniel at Pocomock, Ben, Bull, Jack, Ruiby, the boy Will, Bridget, and Lankaster to him the said Henry Custis his heirs and assigns forever.

ITEM I Give and bequeath unto my two daughters Elizabeth Custis and Sorrowful Margaret Kendall five hundred Acres of Land which I bought of Henry Towles lying and being on Jingoteague Island in Accomack county, together with an Island that I bought of Joh. Morris in the said county containing by estimation three hundred acres of Land, and Marsh, to be held in common between the two Sisters during their natural lives, and after their decease to any two children of their Bodies lawfully begotten. And if it should happen that either of my two daughters should dye without issue, then her part to be and remain to the issue living of either of their Bodies, and their Heirs forever, and in case of failure of any such Heir, then I Give and bequeath the said Land to my son Henry Custis his heir and Assigns forever, the true intent and meaning of this my Will is, if the issue of either or both my said Daughters enter upon the Premises at full age, then they or either of them enjoy the said Land, and their heir forever, my meaning is that my daughters, or their now Husbands give the Land above given to which child they please of my daughters body begotten.

ITEM I Give and bequeath unto my said
daughter

daughter Elizabeth Custis these following Negro Slaves (to wit) George, Sunto, Daniel, her Son, Lucretia, her daughter Yamnone, Indian Sarah, and her son Jemme, and Notse (?) to her during her natural life, and for the life of her Husband Thomas Custis, and after their decease them and their increase I Give to any Child or Children ot their Body lawfully begotten, but for want of any such Issue, then to Thomas Custis her husband, and his heirs forever. Always provided that my now Wife hath the use of the Indian Woman Sarah during her Widowhood.

ITEM I Give and bequeath unto my daughter Sorrowful Margaret Kendall these following Negros or Slaves Nicholas, Jenny his wife, Abigail, Moriah, John a boy, all Children of the said Jenny; Indian Betty, Lettitia, Festus, with all their increase, that they ever shall have, my Negro man named Cesar to her my said daughter during her natural life, and for the life of her Husband William Kendall, and after their decease to be to the issue of the said Sorrowful Margaret Kendall of her body lawfully begotten, to one or more, as she shall think fit, and for want of such Issue, then to the said William Kendall, and his heirs forever.

ITEM I Give to my boy John Atkinson a Horse, four Cows, and Calf, four Ewes, and Lambs, one feather Bed, bolster, one pair of Sheets, two Blankets, and one Rug, and if it should happen that

that I should dye having either Sloop or Sloops, the John Atkinson to take his choice of them, with their Apparel, all which I Give to the said John Atkinson his heirs and assigns forever, but my will is that the said John Adkinson live with my now Wife until he is at the age of one and twenty, unless my now wife cause to the contrary, in whose hands I leave every particular given to be delivered at the aforesaid age or sooner, if she think fit.

ITEM I Give and bequeath unto Sarah Custis Matthews two Cows and two Ewes.

ITEM, I Give and bequeath unto Yardly Michael the remaining part of that Tract of Land, I bought of Joseph Benthall, Senr, him and his heirs forever. Always provided that lives* upon my Plantation at Hungars have liberty to get Timber thereon for the use of this Plantation, I now live on.

ITEM I Give and bequeath unto my daughter Elizabeth Custis my negro man Toney besides what I have here already given her, to her and her heirs forever. Upon mature and deliberate consideration relating to all the Negros and Slaves given to my aforesaid two daughters Elizabeth Custis, and Sorrowful Margaret Kendall, and the more fuller to explain my meaning and will, I do make void the word give, and I do lend the said Negros and Slaves

---

* *Whoever* omitted; or perhaps *my wife while she lives*, as mentioned in an earlier part of this will.

during

during the lives of my said two daughters, and their husbands, and in Case it should happen that either of my said two daughters dye Childless, they shall have liberty to dispose of the said Negros and Slaves to any of their relations as they shall think most fit.

ITEM I Give and bequeath unto my son John Custis, my quarter part of the Brigenteen the Northampton, built by John Bowdoin, and to his Assigns forever, and I likewise give to my said son John Custis, my bigest Silver Tankard, and likewise my father's picture now standing in my Hall.

ITEM I Give to my Wife Sarah Custis, my next largest Silver Tankard.

ITEM I Give and bequeath unto Elias Taylor of Accomack County five hundred acres of Land lying and being at Acaconson in the said County to him and his heirs forever. Always provided, and it is my true intent and meaning that the said Taylor pay to my executors hereafter named, the sum of seventy pounds Sterling by good acceptable Bills of exchange, and fifteen thousand pounds of good Tobacco and cask according to a Verbal agreement made between us which if he refuseth then I do impower my executors hereafte rnamed to make Sale of the said Land for the best advantage they can.

ITEM I Give and bequeath unto Henry Toles [or Joles] of Accomack County and to his heirs

and

and assigns forever five hundred Acres of Land lying and being at Pocomock near Hyleys Neck according to an Agreement made between us, and likewise ten thousand Nails, Always provided that he makes over all his right, title and Interest of five hundred Acres of Land which he lives on: on Jincoteague Island, and acknowledge the same in Accomack County Court to those persons that I [have] given it to by Will, and in the same nature.

ITEM my Will is that before my Estate is divided, these goods hereafter excepted, or the worth of them, be set apart for the use of my now Wife, it being to make her part even of what I have given before to my Children, three feather Beds, Bolsters, & Pillows, three Rugs, three Blankets, to sutes of Curtains and Vallens, ten pair of Sheets, eight pair of pillowbeers, eight Towels, five dozen of Napkins, six Table Cloths, ten pewter dishes, two Basons, three dozen of Plates, one chamber Pot, two Candlesticks, one chafing dish, two Iron Pots, one skillet, one pair of brass and Irons, one pair of fire Tongs, and shovel, one Iron Spitt, one smoothing Iron and Heaters, one dozen of silver Spoons, one Silver Porringer, one large Trunk, covered with Russia Leather, one Sealskin small Trunk marked J. S. C., one Chest that she keeps her Clothes in.

ITEM I Give and Bequeath unto my said Wife all her wearing Apparel both Linen and Woolen
of

of what nature soever they be, and Silks, with all her Rings, Jewells, and a Gold chain, or locket.

ITEM I likewise give to my said Wife Sarah Custis twenty four head of cattle and twenty two Sheep.

ITEM my Will and desire is, that before my Estate is divided, that all my just Debts and Legacies be paid; and that is my desire that my executors make no delay to pay them; all the rest of my Estate I Give and bequeath unto my loving wife Sarah Custis, Hancock Custis, Henry Custis, Elizabeth Custis, Sorrowful Margaret Kendall, to be equally divided. amongst them, whether they be goods, Chattels, Creatures, Moneys or Debts, and upon Division if my Wife have a mind of any particular thing, to have her first choice. I desire my Good friends Captain William Harmanson, George Harmanson, and Mr. Hilary Stringer, to be aiding and assisting my wife and Children to divide my said Estate. I do nominate and appoint my loving wife Sarah Custis, my son Hancock Custis, my son Henry Custis, to be my executors of this my last will & Testament & I do make void all former Wills by me made and Deeds of Gifts whatsoever.

ITEM I give and bequeath unto William Harmanson, Mr. George Harmanson, and Mr. Hilary Stringer each of them a Gold Ring of the value of fifteen shillings apiece to be sent for by my executors.

I give to my sister in law Elishe Frank two cows
and

and cafs and as much Stuff as will [make] her Gown and Petticoat as much new good Linen as will make her three Shifts.

ITEM I give all my wearing apparel to my two Sons Hancock Custis and Henry Custis, of what nature soever to be equally divided amongst them by my now Wife.

ITEM I Give to Robert Housen fifteen shillings to buy him a Gold Ring, to be sent for as aforesaid, and either a Young Mare or Horse. In Testimony that this is my last Will & Testament I have hereunto set my hand and seal this third day of December in the year of our Lord God, one thousand seven hundred and eight.

     JOHN CUSTIS L. S.

 Teste
ROBERT HOUSEN
JOHN SATCHELL
SARAH S P PALMER
  signum
ELISHE FRANK
  her
ELIZABETH X ATKINSON
  mark

Northampton County Ss: March the 16th 17$\frac{10}{11}$.

The said last Will and Testament of John Custis Esqr. was presented to Court by his Relict Mrs. Sarah Custis, his two Sons, Hancock Custis and Henry Custis, his Executors, who made Oath thereto, and upon their motions it is proved in Court by the oaths of Robert Housen, John Satch-
              ell

ell and Elishe Frank, witnesses thereto is admitted to record, and according to order it is recorded.

Teste Robert Housen ⎫ C. Cir^t. Co^t. Nor-
Recorded Teste Robert Housen ⎭   thampton

A Codicil which I annex to this my last will & Testament, and I desire that it be truly and punctually performed as any part of my will whatever.

ITEM That whereas I have in my will given my now dwelling House and Plantation with all the appurtenances thereto belonging, I mean the use of it, to my loving wife Sarah Custis during her natural life, always provided that if she marries that her husband immediately enter into Bond with good Security, as in my said Will is set forth. Now my desire is that if my said Wife should marry, and her Husband refuse to give Bond with Security to my said son Hancock Custis or his heirs, then it shall be lawful for my said Wife to enjoy her thirds, as the law in such Cases provides. Whereas I gave a parcel of Land to Yardly Michael containing three hundred acres whereon he formerly lived, I do revoke that Gift, as if it had never been made, and I do give the said Land with all the advantages thereto belonging, with one hundred Acres of Land thereto belonging to the sole use & Benefit of my now dwelling Plantation to be used by them that are the true Possessors of this my now dwelling Plantation for Timber or otherwise forever. Whereas I have given five hundred Acres
of

of Land on Jingoteague Island in my Will in common as is there expressed, to explain my meaning, my Will and desire is, that my said daughters enjoy the said Land & Negros during their natural lives, and likewise their Husbands, but after their decease, then to go to which Child of their two Bodies lawfully begotten, my said two sons in law, and my daughters, shall think fit, that is if they are not pleased to give it to the eldest, then to any other which they please, still to be held in common: I mean the Land, but the Negros to be distributed amongst my Grand Children as they shall think fit, and whereas I have given my dear wife liberty of range for twenty head of Cattle, on Pocomock, and Gingoteague Island, if she is not pleased to accept of that consideration for her thirds on that Land she may refuse, and then her thirds not to be debared her. this I have writ with my own hand the more to confirm the same.

  Teste.   JOHN CUSTIS L. S.
ROBERT HOUSEN
MATTHEW NEWMAN
SARAH CUSTIS × MATTHEWS
   signum.

And my desire is, and I will and bequeath to my dear wife all the grain of what sort soever shall be founed on my Plantation either in growing in the field or lying in the Houses, together with all my Hogs for her support, and my will and desire is that the smith Tools I shall be or am possessed with
              the

shall go, and I give them to my daughter, Elizabeth Custis, and her heirs forever, and my will is that the Male Cattle given to my son John Custis in my will, bars him of any further claim I owed him of nineteen head, and I owed for the exchange of his part from Pocomock, being I am sensible many more; and my will and desire is that my girl Abigail that I formerly gave to my daughter Margaret in my Will be and remain with all her increase to my grandson Custis Kendall and his heirs and assigns forever. Whereas I am sensible of my interlinings in my Will all that can be thought of my writing or Mr. Housens, I do confirm, and desire that this part of my Codicil with the rest may be perpetually performed. Signed, Sealed and acknowledged as the part or Codicil annexed to my will before

JOHN CUSTIS L. S.

JOHN ATKINSON
ELIZABETH FOX } Witnesses.
ROBERT HOUSEN

March the 20th 17$\frac{1}{1}$

Upon consideration of a late Act of Assembly made at Williamsburgh the last Sessions, my Will and desire is that none of my Estate be appraised as the law set forth, but that my Estate as formerly given in this my will and Codicil hereto annexed be divided accordingly, and every one to enjoy his part in special I will hope my Estate will not be in debt, to this I set my hand, and the Day and year above

above written. The Pistols I design for my son John, I have sent them to him.

JOHR CUSTIS, L. S.

Nor my executors to give Security

JOHN CUSTIS, L. S.

Signed, sealed & acknowledged
as my act and Deed as a Codicil
annexed to my Will amongst
the other Codicils before inserted

>ROBERT HOUSEN
>>Signum
>
>PHILIP P. H. HAMMON
>>Signum
>
>WILLIAM N. BANUM
>>Signum
>
>BATT N. NOTTINGHAM

Northampton County, Sc. March the 16th, 17$\frac{1}{1}$.

The said three Codicils of John Custis, Esqr, dec'd, being annexed to his said last will and Testament was also presented in Court by his said Executors with the said Will and upon their motion the said three Codicils was like wise proved in Court by the Oaths of Robert Housen, Sarah Custis Matthews, John Atkinson, Elizabeth Fox, Philip Hammon, Batt Nottingham, witnesses thereto, is admitted to record, and according to order, it is recorded.

Teste, Robert Housen ⎫ C. Cir^t C^t Nor-
Recorded Teste, Robert Housen ⎭ thampton.

Copies Teste

GRIFFIN STITH, Cl. N. C.

INDEX.

Abingdon, 86.
Accokeek, 46n, 59, 75.
Accomac county, 186.
Adams, Daniel Jenifer, 130.
    Francis, 161.
    Gabriel, 43.
    John Quincy, 109.
    Robert, 160.
Alexander, Robert, 93n.
Alexander the Great, victories of, 160.
Alexandria, 77.
    Academy, bequest to, 87n.
    Bank, 88, 139.
    lots in, 84, 134.
    near, 113.
Alt, Theophilus, 108n.
Alton, John, 105.
Anderson, David, 13.
Appleton, John, 18.
Arlington House, 185.
Ashby's Bent, 122.
Ashton, Ann(Washington),114.
    Burdet, 115n.
    Sarah, 115n.
Athenæum, Boston, 98n.
Atkinson, John, 189, 190, 197.
    Elizabeth, 194.
    George, 167.

Augusta Academy, 93n.
Aylett, Ann, 41. See *Ann Washington*.

Bailey, J., 107.
Ball, Burges, 63, 67, 69, 116n.
    Frances (Washington),61, 116.
    George Washington, 70n.
    Joseph, 62.
    Mary, 43. See *Mary Washington*.
Balridge, 36.
Bank of Alexandria, 88, 139.
    Columbia, 139.
Banks, Henry, 143n.
Banum, William, 198.
Barrow, Alexander, 27.
    John B., 28.
Bassett, Frances, 111n. See *Lewis*.
Bath, 123, 136.
Baylor, Robert W., 170.
Baynham, Alexander, 10n.
Beall, Eliza R., 154n.
Benthall, Joseph, 190.
Berkeley county, 93, 122.
Berkham, 158.
Berrien, John, 102n.
Bet, negro, 60.

(199)

200

Betty, negro, 47.
Bible, Washington's, 103.
Biddle, Clement, Lear's letter to, 87n.
    Washington's letter to, 86n.
Bishop, Thomas, 105.
Blackburn, Ann, 151.
    Ann Maria, 154n.
    JaneCharlotte,154n, 173.
    Richard, 161.
    Richard Scott,173n.
    Thomas, 151n, 161.
Botetourt county, 128n, 141.
Bowdoin, John, 191.
Box, Earl of Buchan's, 99, 100n.
Bradwater, William, 186.
Bridge, Anthony, 12.
Bridge Creek, 44, 62n.
Buchan, Earl of, 99, 100.
Bullskin, 74, 76, 94n, 122.
Burning Spring, 128.
Burwell, Lewis, 97n.
Bushrod, Hannah, 43. See *Hannah Washington*.
Busts, 160.
Butler, Caleb, 19.
    Lawrence, 34, 35.
Byrd, William, lottery of, 97.

Canes, Washington, 102.
Capteeuing Creek, 126n.
Carlyle, John, 78, 104.
    Sarah, 104.

Carolaca, 131.
Carter, Betty (Lewis), 60, 61, 63, 67, 97, 115.
    Charles, 67, 69, 97.
    Charles (the elder), 98n.
Cary, Wilson Miles, 104n.
Chambers, 115n.
Chapman, James, 102.
    Nathaniel, 49, 78.
Charles county, Md., 130.
Charson, Henry L., 144.
Chattin's Run, 122.
Chew, John, 62.
Chincoteague, 168, 192, 196.
Chotank, 42, 44, 50, 101.
Clinton, George, 99, 131.
Cole, Mr., 9n.
Cole River, 128, 143.
Collard, Samuel, 162.
Congress, New York Provincial, 102n.
Conoway, Christopher, 42n.
Conway, Moncure D., 42n, 60.
Corner, William H., 103n, 104n.
Coxe, Daniel, 131.
Coxeborough, 131.
Craik, Dr. James, 102.
Crane, Samuel J., 178.
Crask, Edmund, 29.
Crawford, William, 131n.
Cresap, Col., 75, 76, 126n.
Cruttwell, Clement, 103n.
Culpepper, Thomas, 12n.
Cunningham, Ann Pamelia 177.

201

Custis, Eleanor Parke, 112, 113, 116. See *Lewis*.
    Elizabeth, 188, 189, 190, 193, 197.
    George Washington Parke, 51*n*, 102*n*, 112, 113, 117, 119.
    Hancock, 183, 184, 185, 186, 187, 193, 194, 195.
    Henry, 187, 188, 193, 194.
    John, will of, 183.
    John, 185, 187, 191, 198.
    John Parke, 102*n*, 105*n*, 117*n*.
    Nellie (Calvert), 102*n*, 105*n*, 117*n*.
    Sarah, 183, 184, 186, 191, 192, 193, 194, 195.

Dandridge, Bartholomew, 95, 96.
    John, 95, 96, 124*n*.
    Mary, 96.
Darke, William, 110*n*.
Davis, Pierce, 186.
De Butts, Lawrence, 9*n*.
Deep Creek, 62*n*.
    Run, 42, 43, 45, 62*n*.
Deneale, G., 9, 140.
Difficult Bridge, 121.
    Run, 99.
Dinwiddie, Gov., 127*n*.
Dismal Swamp, 99, 125.
    Company, 126*n*, 151.

District of Columbia, University for, 92.
Dogue Run, 73, 109, 111, 113.
Dorsey, James, 153.
Dower negroes, 84.
Dudley, William, 12*n*, 13*n*.
Dumfries, 63*n*.
Dunmore, Lord, 127*n*, 128*n*.

Edenburgh, 98.
Edwards, Meridah, 35.
Education, Washington on, 90.
Ellenborough, Lord, 116*n*.
Emmet, Thomas Addis, 155*n*.
England, John, 46.
Epsewasson Creek, 13*n*.
Erskine, David Stuart, 99*n*.
Ernst, O. H., 134*n*.
Essex County, 23*n*.
Estaing, 161*n*.
Evan's Mountain, 122.

Fairfax, Bryan, Lord, 103, 104*n*.
    George William, 78.
    William, 78.
Fairfax County, 12*n*, 71, 75.
Fairfield, 105.
Falmouth, 62*n*.
Fincastle County, 128*n*.
Finch, Thomas, 50.
Fitzhugh, William, of Chatham, 97*n*.
Flagg, Henry, 11.
Fleming, Alexander, 24*n*, 25*n*, 26.

Fleming, Jane or Joyce, 24*n*,
    25*n*, 101*n*.
    Ursula, 24*n*, 25*n*.
Forbach, Madame de, 101*n*.
Ford, West, 161.
Foster, Robert, 14.
Four mile run, 86*n*, 113.
Foxall, John, 12.
Fox, Elizabeth, 197, 198.
Foxcraft, Isaac, 186.
Frank, negro, 41.
Frank, Elishe, 194, 195.
Franklin's cane, 101.
Frederick, negro, 60.
Frederick County, 74, 75, 123.
Fredericksburg, 46*n*, 50, 59, 62,
    63, 66, 97.
Fries, John, 14.

Ganst's engravings, 160*n*.
George, negro, 59.
Gibson, Mrs. Mary (Washington), 26*n*. See *Mary Washington*.
Giles, Captain, 12*n*.
Gloucester County, 99, 123.
Goldsmith's company, 99*n*, 100.
Goose Creek, 77.
Gordon, Samuel, 98.
Gound, 78.
Grant, Margaret, 42*n*.
Gray, John, 51*n*.
Great Meadows, 131.
Green, Sarah, 101.
    William, 12*n*, 13*n*.

Gregory, Roger, 35*n*, 36*n*.

Hammon, Philip, 198.
Hammond, Mildred (Washington), 116.
    Thomas, 116*n*.
Hampshire County, 123.
Harewood, 110*n*.
Harmanson, George, 193.
    William, 193.
Harrison, Mr., 131*n*.
    Benjamin, 129*n*.
    George, 45*n*.
    Maria Powell, 154*n*.
    Nathaniel, Jr., 97*n*.
    William, 45*n*.
Harvie, John, 126*n*.
Hawkins, Thomas, 27.
Hayden, Rev. Horace Edwin,
    19*n*, 24*n*, 25*n*, 26*n*, 116*n*, 117*n*.
Hayfield, 105.
Haynie, Elizabeth, 105.
    Sallie Ball, 105.
Hedges, Robert, 11.
Herbert, Bushrod W., 159, 164, 165.
    Edward, 104*n*.
    James R., 104*n*.
    John C., 104*n*.
    Mary Lee, 155, 158, 159, 164, 166, 167.
    Noblet, 161, 164.
    Thomas, 104*n*.
    William, 104*n*.
Hills, Richard, 13, 36.
Holland, John, 10*n*.

Hood, John, 98.
Horton, William, 9*n*.
Houdon, 160*n*.
Housen, Robert, 194, 195, 196, 197, 198.
Howard, 25.
Howes, Thomas, 20, 38.
Hungars, 183, 190.
Hutchinson, David, 104*n*.
Hyley's neck, 192.

Ingle, Henry and Joseph, 118*n*.
Inglis, Rev. Mr., 103.

Jackson, Andrew, 102*n*.
    Robert, 49, 50.
    S., 109*n*.
James River shares, 89, 92, 139.
Johnson, Dennis, 168.
Jones, John Paul, 160.
    Mary, 23*n*, 101*n*.
Jordan, Thomas, 14.
Judy, negro, 47.

Kanhawa lands, 99.
Kendall, Custis, 197.
    Sorrowful M., 188, 189, 190, 193.
    Wm., 187, 189.
Kentucky, lands in, 132.
Keys, Gersham, 77.
King George County, 12*n*, 41, 46*n*.
King's College telescope, 102*n*.
Kittoctan, 130.
Lafayette, 103, 160*n*.

Lancashire furnace, 46*n*.
Lancaster County, 23*n*, 26*n*.
Lands, Western, 118, 126, 141.
Langhorn, Mary, 24*n*.
Law, Elizabeth Parke, 116.
Lear, Frances, 105.
    Tobias, 87*n*, 105, 112.
Le Brun, 160*n*.
Lee, Cassius F., 135*n*.
    Edmund I., 177, 178.
    George, 53*n*.
    Hannah, 154*n*.
    Ludwell, 140.
    Mary, 114*n*.
    Richard Henry, 114*n*, 154*n*.
    William, 86, 87*n*.
Lewis, Andrew, 130.
    Betty (Washington), 45, 46, 59, 61, 63, 76, 97*n*, 112, 115.
    George, 106, 110*n*.
    Eleanor Parke (Custis), 116.
    Elizabeth, 34.
    Fielding, 60, 97*n*.
        Jr., 115, 125.
    George, 115, 152, 155, 166.
    Howell, 115.
    John, 34*n*.
    Laurence, 60, 107, 112, 113, 117, 119, 140, 162.
    Robert, 63, 115.
    Thomas, 43, 146.
    Virginia T., 109*n*.

Lewis. Warner, 124*n*.
Liberty Hall, 93.
Liston, Daniel, 36.
    Robert, 36, 37.
Little, Charles, 140.
Little Hunting Creek, 13*n*, 36, 41, 73, 109, 111, 112, 155,
Lord, John, 18.
Lossing, Benson J., 107, 119*n*, 161*n*.
Loudoun county, 99, 121.
Lydia, negro, 60.

Macaulay, Mrs., 103*n*.
Machoactoke River, 9*n*, 12, 36.
Manchester, lots in, 97.
Mansion House, 111.
Markham, Lewis, 36.
Marshall, John, 98, 163.
Maruim, Lewis, 11.
Mary, negro, 47.
Maryland, property in, 130.
Mason, George, 161.
    Thomson, 97*n*, 98*n*, 110, 113, 155, 166.
Mattox, 36, 43, 45, 47, 48.
McCarty, Daniel, 49.
Meade, Bishop, 29*n*.
    Richard Kidder, 97*n*.
Mercer, John Francis, 123, 130*n*.
    James, 61, 64, 70.
    Sophia, 130*n*.
Miami River, lands on, 132.
Michael, Yardley, 190.
Micou, James Roy, 29.

Millan, George, 168.
Minton, Elizabeth, 36.
Moll, negro, 74, 76.
Montgomery county, Md., 130.
Moratico, 62*n*.
Morris, John, 188.
Moseley, Capt. Wm., 26.
Moss, Alfred, 141.
    William, 168.
Mottrom, John, 13*n*.
Mount Vernon estate, 12, 36*n*, 41, 53*n*, 73, 108, 151, 153, 155, 157, 176.
Muddy hole, 110.
Mumford, George W., 141.
Mumford's Museum, 161.

Nansemond county, 125.
Necker, bust of, 160.
Necostin's town, 9*n*.
Negroes, dower, 84.
Newman, Matthew, 196.
New York, property in, 131.
Nicholas, Lewis, 35.
Nore, James, 45.
North, John, 78.
Northumberland County, 14, 18*n*, 26*n*.
Norway, David, 13.
Nottingham, Batt, 198.
Nugent, James, 155, 156.

Ohio company, 77.
    lands, 126.

Pace, Alexia, 25*n*.

Pace, Jane, 25n.
    Thomas, 25n.
Page, John, 98n.
Palmer, Sarah, 194.
Parish, Truro, 12.
    Washington, 9, 16, 33, 35.
Parishes in Virginia, formation of, 9n.
Parks, Harriot (Washington), 115.
    Andrew, 115n.
Peake, Humphrey, 111, 153, 161.
Pendergrass, Gerrard, 75, 76.
Pendleton, Edmund, 53, 63n.
    Philip, 93, 94.
Pennsylvania, property in, 131.
Peter, Martha Parke, 116.
Phil, gardener, 159.
Pipe Creek, 126n.
Piscatoway Indian town, 12n.
Pope, Anne, 11, 15, 17, 19. See *Ann Washington*.
    Thomas, 11, 14n, 17.
Pope's Creek, 51.
Porter & Coates, 103n.
Posey, Thomas, 128n.
Potomac river, 9n, 12n, 13n.
    shares, 89, 92, 138.
Prince George County, 98n.
    William County, 12n, 41, 43, 45, 47, 48, 53, 54.
Principio Iron Company, 42, 45, 75, 76.

Randolph, Edmund, 129n.
    Peter, 98n.
    Peyton, 97n, 98n.
    Richard, 97n.
Rappahannock creek, 13.
    County, 23n.
Redman, Robert, 38.
Richards, Robert, 14.
Richardson, F. W., 141n, 169.
Richmond, 97.
    County, 23n.
Riggs, Alice L., 108.
Robertson, Archibald, 100.
Robinson, John, 98n.
    Maxim, 77.
Rogers, Edmund Law, 117n.
Rosier, John, 12, 38.
Rosier's Creek, 11.
Rough Creek, 132.
Round Bottom, 126.
    Hill, 9n, 36.
Rumsey, James, 136n.
Rush, William, 36.

Salisbury Plains, 74, 77.
Sandy, Henry, Jr., 28.
Saratoga, 132n.
Satchell, John, 194, 195.
Simms, Charles, 140.
Slaves, Washington's, 84, 96.
Sodor and Man, Bishop of, 103.
Sparks, Jared, 98n.
Spencer, Francis, 13n, 45n.
    Nicholas, 10n, 12, 13n.
Spotswood, Elizabeth (Washington), 114.

Spotswood, Alexander, 114*n*, 154*n*.
    General A., 132.
Spotsylvania County, 59.
Spy-glass, Washington's, 102.
Stafford County, 12, 36, 42, 59.
Stewart, James, 130*n*.
    Rebecca, 130*n*.
Stith, Griffin, 198.
Stock, live, 139.
Stocks, United States, 137.
Storkes quarter, 37.
Story, Judge Joseph, 161.
Strickland, 119*n*.
Stringer, Hilary, 193.
Strother, Anthony, 49, 50, 51.
    William, 42.
Struthers, John, 119*n*.
Stuart, David, 102, 105*n*, 141.
    Eleanor (Custis), 105.
    Mr., 77.
Sue, negro, 47.
Summers, George W., 106*n*.
    Samuel, 156.
Swords, Washington, 106.

Taylor, 114*n*.
    Elias, 191.
Telescope, King's College, 102*n*.
Thomas, Margaret (Lee), 87*n*.
Thomazine, John, 25*n*.
Thomson, James, 49, 50, 51.
Thompson, Samuel, 34, 37.
    William, 34.
Thornton, Elizabeth, 25*n*.

Thornton, Jane, 114.
    Mildred, 43*n*.
    Presley, 98*n*.
    Rowland, 25*n*.
    Col. —., 114*n*.
    Lieut., 128*n*.
Tiffy, Mathew, 50.
Tom, negro, 59.
Towles, Henry, 188, 191.
Townshend, Frances, 24*n*.
    Mary, 24*n*, 101.
    Mary (Langhorne), 24*n*.
    Robert, 24*n*.
Truro Parish, 12*n*, 73.
Trumbull, Charles, 98*n*.
Turner, Harry, 151.
    —., 51.

United States Stocks, 137.

Vault, family, 73, 118.

Wahanganoche, 18.
Waite, William, 78.
Wakefield, 36*n*, 51*n*.
Wales, John, 97*n*.
Walker, Ann, 105.
    Joseph, 61, 62.
    Thomas, 125.
Wallace, William, 99.
Waller, John, 50.
Walpole grant, 127*n*.
Warm Springs, 123, 136.
Warner, Elizabeth, 34*n*.
    Mildred, 35.

Warren, Andrew W., 78.
Washington, Ann (daughter of John), 14, 15, 16, 17, 34.
    Ann (daughter of Laurence), 24, 25, 101n.
    Ann (Fairfax), 53n, 73.
    Ann (m. *Ashton*), 114.
    Ann (Blackburn), 151.
    Ann Eliza, 167.
    Ann Maria, 175, 178n.
    Augustine (son of Lawrence), 35, 36, 42n, 46n, 47n, 51, 53; will of, 41.
    Augustine (son of Augustine), 41, 45, 47, 48, 49, 51n, 53, 75, 76, 78, 115.
    Betty, 45, 46. See *Lewis*.
    Bushrod, 53n, 67, 68, 98, 106, 107, 108, 113, 116, 119, 151, 176; will of, 151.
    Bushrod (of Mt. Zephyr), 154, 156, 157, 158,
    159, 161, 162, 165, 167.
Washington, Bushrod Corbin, 154, 158, 159, 162, 167, 177, 178.
    Charles, 43, 44, 48, 54, 59, 64, 75, 76, 101, 116.
    Charles Augustine, [111], 112n, 116.
    Corbin, 59, 116, 154, 155.
    Elizabeth, 114n.
    Elizabeth (Foote), 105.
    Ella Bassett, 109.
    Ferdinand, 115n.
    Frances, 116.
    George, 36n, 42, 44, 47, 48, 50, 51, 52, 53n, 59, 61, 62n, 75, 76, 78, 127n, 152, 155, 160, 161, 163, 166; death and burial, 118n; letter to Mrs. Lewis, 63, 68; letter to Ba¹ and Carter, 53 letter to Bushrod, W., 98n; letter to Chambers, 115n; let-

ter to Warner
Lewis, 124; let-
ter to Jno. Har-
vie, 126n; let-
ter to E. Ran-
dolph, 129n;
letter to Clin-
ton, 132n; let-
ter to D. Stuart,
141; letter of
Banks, 143n;
swords of, 108n;
will of, 83.

Washington, George Augus-
tine, 60, 67, 111,
116.
George Corbin,
51n, 106n, 109n,
154, 155, 156,
157, 158, 159,
160, 161, 162.
George Fayette,
111, 116.
George Steptoe,
94, 106, 108,
110n, 115, 119,
140.
George W., 167,
168.
Hannah (Bush-
rod), 43, 59, 104.
Hannah (Fairfax),
105.
Harriet, 115.
Jane (Fleming),
24, 27.

Washington, Jane, 114n, 116;
m. Washington.
Jane, 114; m.
Thornton.
Jane C., 119, 163,
173, 176, 177.
Jane Mildred, 167.
John (immigrant),
10, 12n, 13n,
14n, 19, 26n,
27, 51n; will of,
9.
John (son of John),
11, 13, 14, 15,
17, 34.
John (son of im-
migrant Law-
rence), 16, 24,
25, 25n, 27, 35,
37, 51n, 101n.
John (son of John
2d), 24n, 101n.
John (son of Law-
rence 2d), 36,
37.
John Augustine,
. 43, 44, 48, 54,
62n, 64, 75, 76,
77, 104n, 114n.
John Augustine,
152, 154, 158,
159, 160, 162,
163, 165, 167,
168, will of, 173.
Lawrence (immi-
grant), 14, 16,

17, 23, 24, 25,
101*n*; will of,
23.
Washington, Lawrence (son of
immigrant
John), 11, 12,
13*n*, 15, 16, 17,
33, 51*n*; will of,
33.
Lawrence (son of
Augustine), 41,
43, 45, 46, 47,
48, 49, 51, 53;
will of, 73.
Lawrence (son of
John), 35, 101,
102.
Lawrence Augustine, 94, 110*n*,
[111], 112*n*, 115.
Lawrence Augustine, 2d, 110*n*.
Lewis William,
51*n*, 109*n*.
Lund, 65, 94*n*,
101*n*, 105*n*.
Maria, 116.
Martha, 17.
Martha (Dandridge), 83, 95,
119.
Martha D., 110*n*.
Mary (Ball), 43,
63, will of, 59.
Mary (Jones), 23*n*,
101*n*.

Mary (Townshend), 24*n*.
Washington, Mary (*m.* Gibson),
23, 24, 25*n*, 27,
101*n*.
Mary Lee, 155.
Mildred (Warner),
35, 38.
Mildred (*m.* Gregory-Willis,) 35,
36.
Mildred (*m.* Hammond), 116.
Mildred (*m.*
Thornton), 43*n*,
61, 105.
Richard B., 178.
Richard Henry
Lee, 164.
Robert, 101.
Samuel (son of
Augustine), 42,
43, 44, 48, 50,
54, 62*n*, 64, 75,
76, 93, 94, 112.
Samuel (son of
Charles), 101*n*,
106*n*, 107*n*, 110,
116, 119, 140.
Samuel T., 101*n*,
106*n*.
Sarah, 54, 74, 75,
76, 78.
Thornton, 93, 94,
115.
Thornton A., 110*n*.

Washington, Townsend, 101*n*.
    Warner, 105*n*.
    William Augustine, 51*n*, 97, 106, 109*n*, 114, 119, 154*n*.
Washington Academy, 93*n*.
Washington and Lee University, 93.
Washington city, lots in, 114, 133.
Washington Parish, 9*n*.
Water mill, 11, 37, 41, 47, 155.
Waters, Henry F., 13*n*.
Watts, —., 11.
Webb, William, 36.
Weedon, Captain George, 127*n*.
    George, 38.
Weeks, Benjamin, 50.
Welles, Albert, 29*n*.
Westcomb, James, 20, 38.
West, Falco, 26.
Westmoreland County, 9*n*, 18*n*, 33, 41, 43, 50, 53.
White, Daniel, 35.
Whitely, Henry, 47*n*.
Whitmore, William H., 29.

Whittsons, John, 13.
Wickeff, Henry, 20.
Will of George Washington, original, 141*n*.
Willet, Marinus, 131.
Willett, William, 185.
William. See *William Lee*.
Williams, Mrs., 36.
Willie, William, 98.
Willis, Col. Henry, 35*n*, 50.
Wilmot, Henry, 102*n*.
Wilson, Thomas, 103.
    Col., 77.
Winchester, lots in, 135.
Winneberger, 119*n*.
Withers, Edmund, 42*n*.
    John, 42*n*.
    Sarah, 42*n*.
    Thomas, 42*n*.
    William, 42*n*.
Wood, Cornelius, 28.
    John, 97*n*.
Woodstock Manor, 130*n*.
Wormley's line, 122.
Wright, Major Francis, 14*n*, 37.
Wythe, George, 97*n*.

PUBLICATIONS

OF THE

Historical Printing Club,

97 CLARK ST.,

The Sayings of Poor Richard.

THE PREFACES, PROVERBS AND POEMS OF
BENJAMIN FRANKLIN,

ORIGINALLY PRINTED IN

POOR RICHARD'S ALMANACS, 1733-1758.

EDITED BY
PAUL LEICESTER FORD.

Octavo, pp. 288, 9 plates, half morocco, gilt top, uncut.
Only 100 copies printed.
Price, $5.00.

Though the sayings of Poor Richard have enjoyed a world-wide reputation, this is the first time they have ever been collected from the excessively rare original almanacs, as well as their first appearance in a volume. This large paper edition contains seven photographic illustrations not in the ordinary edition, and has been printed and bound to range with Bigelow's edition of Franklin's writings, to which it forms a necessary supplementary volume.

"Published in a more elegant style than their author ever imagined possible."
—*New York Observer.*

"This reprint of Poor Richard's Proverbs, Poems and Epigrams is a better commentary on Franklin and his times than could be had in the most labored historical essays."—*St. Louis Republic.*

"Both the compiler and publishers deserve thanks for placing writings, highly interesting both in themselves and historically, in so attractive and convenient a form."—*Boston Advertiser.*

"A gem of Colonial Literature."—*Brooklyn Eagle.*

Letters of Joseph Jones,

OF VIRGINIA.

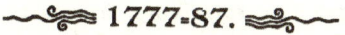 1777-87.

EDITED BY
WORTHINGTON C. FORD.

Small 4to., pp. xiv, 157.
Only 250 copies printed.
Price, in sheets stitched, uncut, $5.00.
In cloth, uncut, $6.00.

These letters, now for the first time printed, form a most important mass of historical material treating of revolutionary and subsequent events. The writer, Joseph Jones, was a member of the Virginia House of Burgesses, of the State Convention of 1776, of the Continental Congress and the State Convention of 1788. Among his correspondents were Washington, Madison, and Jefferson, and his abilities and surrounding make his opinions and information of interest and value.

Pamphlets on the Constitution of the United States.

PUBLISHED DURING ITS DISCUSSION BY THE PEOPLE.

1787—8.

EDITED WITH NOTES AND A BIBLIOGRAPHY BY

PAUL LEICESTER FORD.

Large Octavo. 451 Pages. Only 500 Copies Printed.
Price, Half Morocco, Gilt Top, uncut, $6.00.
Cloth, Gilt Top, uncut, $5.00.

This is a reprint of rare pamphlets, written on our Constitution during the time that government was under discussion prior to its acceptance by the people. These pamphlets are of much importance for the history of that period, and an examination of the originals would necessitate visits to Washington, Philadelphia, New York and Boston, and "take a lifetime of patient searching and waiting to collect them from the second-hand booksellers and auction rooms, at prices that few would care to pay." As a consequence they have hitherto been almost unknown as historical material. They are as follows:

[GERRY, ELBRIDGE]. Observations on the New Constitution, and on the Federal and State Conventions. By a Columbian Patriot.

[WEBSTER, NOAH]. An examination into the leading principles of the Federal Constitution. By a citizen of America.

[JAY, JOHN]. An Address to the People of the State of New York, on the subject of the Constitution. By a Citizen of New York.

[SMITH, MELANCTHON]. Address to the People of the State of New York. By a Plebeian.
[WEBSTER, PELATIAH]. The weakness of Brutus exposed; or some remarks in vindication of the Constitution. By a Citizen of Philadelphia.
[COXE, TENCH]. An examination of the Constitution of the United States of America. By an American Citizen.
WILSON, JAMES. Speech on the Federal Constitution, delivered in Philadelphia.
[DICKINSON, JOHN]. Letters of Fabius on the Federal Constitution.
[HANSON, ALEXANDER CONTEE]. Remarks on the Proposed Plan of a Federal Government. By Aristides.
RANDOLPH, EDMUND. Letters on the Federal Constitution.
[LEE, RICHARD HENRY]. Observations on the System of Government proposed by the late Convention. By a Federal Farmer.
MASON, GEORGE. Objections to the Federal Constitution.
[IREDELL, JAMES]. Observations on George Mason's Objections to the Federal Constitution. By Marcus.
[RAMSAY, DAVID]. An Address to the Freemen of South Carolina on the Federal Constitution. By Civis.
Bibliography of the Constitution, 1787-1789. By the Editor.

"A happy thought to reproduce in this centennial period a select number of the pamphlets which were published for or against the Constitution. . . . gathered from the wide field of political pamphleteering in 1787 and 1788, we can hear the political accent of the living age in almost every variety of tone, and can catch, as from a phonograph, the true and false emphasis which was then peculiar to the political dialect of the country."—*The Nation.*

"The fourteen *Pamphlets on the Constitution* . . . form a valuable addition to the literature of American Constitutional law and history. The Bibliography and reference list at the end are especially useful."—*The New York Tribune.*

THE WASHINGTON-DUCHÉ LETTERS,

Now printed for the first time, from the original manuscripts, with an introductory note by

WORTHINGTON CHAUNCEY FORD.

Small Quarto, pp. 38. Only 500 copies printed. Price, $1.50.

"It is not a little surprising to discover that this famous letter has never been known *as it was written*, but only from imperfect copies published in channels where garbling had become a recognized trade. . . . On Nov. 29, 1777, in one of the early issues of Rivington's *Gazette*, was published this letter, and soon after it was included in a pamphlet issued from the same press, appended to the "Forged Letters" of Washington. . . . It again appeared with the Spurious Letters of 1796, but still retaining the Rivington text, of which the editor of the *Official Letters* of Washington to Congress wrote: 'I regret extremely that I cannot. (without openly avowing myself the author) point out to the public the prodigious incorrectness of Mr. Duché's letter. Having compared it with a correct copy which I have taken from the files, I find no less than *one hundred and forty deviations* from the genuine text:—in which number I do not count orthography and punctuation.' When Mr. Sparks was making up his important collection of letters written to Washington during the Revolution, he used the Rivington version, and his example was followed by the compiler of Washington at Valley Forge."—*Preface.*

In addition to the Duché and Washington letters, this volume contains Washington's letter to Francis Hopkinson, and Hopkinson's to Duché, concerning this letter; and Duché's letter, written after the signing of the treaty of peace in 1783, with Washington's reply.

THE SPURIOUS LETTERS

ATTRIBUTED TO

WASHINGTON.

EDITED BY

WORTHINGTON CHAUNCEY FORD.

Quarto, pp. 166, paper, uncut.
Only 500 copies printed.
Price $3.00.

This volume contains the famous "forged" letters which were published in England and America in 1777 with a design to undermine the influence of Washington and depict him as a traitor to the cause he was leading. An attempt to establish the authorship is here first made, and many illustrations from the genuine letters of the General are given to show how closely the fabricator of the spurious letters imitated the thoughts and even the style of the supposed writer. Some rare and curious biographical sketches of Washington, printed during his life-time are added, with other material of a like nature.

One hundred copies of the tract contain a reproduction of a letter from John Randolph, the last royal Attorney-General of Virginia, and the supposed forger. Price, $4.00.

The Origin, Purpose and Result

OF THE

HARRISBURG CONVENTION OF 1788

BY
PAUL LEICESTER FORD.

Quarto, pp. 40, paper, uncut.
Only 250 copies printed.
Price, $1.00.

The Harrisburg Convention was described by its contemporaries a a "smuggling business," and to this day its original purpose has been i doubt, as indeed much of its history. To clear up the objects and result of this secret gathering, the greatest pains have been taken to embody a information, both printed and manuscript, bearing on it. From the ma ter thus for the first time brought to light, it appears almost certain tha this meeting of prominent Pennsylvanians, such as William Findley, Georg Bryan, John Smiley, Albert Gallatin, and many others, who were united i their opposition to the Federal Constitution, was held for the purpose c preventing the organization of the United States Government, or if poss ble to secure the secession of such counties of the State as were oppose to that government; and as the first attempt at nullification or secessior deserves more prominence in our histories than has as yet been accorde to it.

www.ingramcontent.com/pod-product-compliance
Lightning Source LLC
Chambersburg PA
CBHW031832230426
43669CB00009B/1318